Sydney

Footprint

Darroch Donald

KT-415-620

Contents

Listings

About the author

Scot Darroch Donald has two major passions in life: wildlife and travel. After gaining a diploma in wildlife illustration and photography, Darroch took up the position of assistant manager at a wildlife rehabilitation center in Scotland. This work took him to many far-flung places, including Saudi Arabia during the Gulf War eco-disaster in 1991 and eventually to New Zealand, where he emigrated in 1992. There he acted as an oiled wildlife consultant to the government and in 1996 published his first book, *Creatures*, an account of his wildlife encounters. In 1998 Darroch crossed the Tasman to live in Sydney. Now Darroch has expanded his work to include both travel and nature. He is co-author of Footprint's Australia Handbook and author of Footprint's New Zealand Handbook.

Acknowledgements

Darroch Donald would like to thank all the staff and representatives of the Sydney and Sydney Region Visitor Information Centres and regional tourism offices who provided invaluable advice and assistance. Also, a huge thanks to Jacki Sawkeld and Libby Hall in Sydney, Sally Van Natta and Tony and Brigitte in Santa Barbara, California, for their invaluable help, valued friendship and for providing sanctuary from the rigours of the road. Thanks too to all the team at Footprint and Alan Murphy and Rachel Fielding in particular for their much appreciated patience, support and hard work. Special mention also to Katrina and Swaff for their friendship, help, enthusiasm and unfaltering commitment to the job. Finally a special thanks, as ever, to my mother Grace for her steadfast encouragement and support, to my brother Ghill for assisting with frequent cashflow problems and for the many tonic email attachments and to my partner Rebecca, who knows that although she is unable to join me on the road is always with me in my thoughts and in my heart.

Introducing Sydney

Once seen as isolated, parochial and immature, Sydney has grown up to become spectacular, brash, colourful, hedonistic and a major world destination. Arranged intricately around the coves and beaches of an enormous and convoluted natural harbour, the city is home to almost a quarter of Australia's population. In January 1788 Captain Arthur Phillip, commander of the 'First Fleet', weighed anchor in Port Jackson. With a modicum of arrogance, and ignoring the local Aboriginal proclamations of 'Warra Warra' (meaning, approximately, 'bugger off'), he declared the entire continent a British penal colony. Now, where once stood a conglomerate of sorry-looking shacks and lock-ups full of bedraggled convicts, stands a forest of glistening high rises. In the shadows of these shiny pieces of modernity stroll cosmopolitan hordes of workers, proud of their welcoming and vibrant city. Lauded as the 'real' (though not administrative) capital of a harsh and colossal continent and an economic and political focal point of the southern hemisphere, Sydney is a sexy city.

Olympic gold

The 2000 Olympics only added to the city's reputation and its architectural wealth. Record-breaking amounts of money were spent on inner-city rejuvenation, transportation and modern sports venues, providing the infrastructure and the stage for what were dubbed the best games ever. Many cynics expected a huge slump after the great global event – some kind of 'post-traumatic hype disorder' – but it never occurred. Baked to perfection under the Aussie sun, with a sweet topping of sea, surf and culture, it seems Sydney life just went back to normal.

Problems, icons and matchsticks

Sure, the city has its problems and in some ways is just like any other: drugs (the dark side of its glamorous party image), crime, bushfires and a ceaseless urban sprawl. There is an arrogant tendency to forget the city's relationship with the mighty continent and the superficially seamless cosmopolitan mix has hidden fractiousness. Take away the instantly recognisable icons of the Opera House, the harbour and the mighty bridge, call the place 'Bob' and things might be different. Sydney, however, has a great deal more to offer: fascinating museums and art galleries, international cuisine, surfing beaches, world-renowned festivals, 24-hour entertainment, state-of-the-art sports venues and a whole host of exciting activities. Then there are some of its lesser-known secrets: its colony of outrageously big bats, a talking dog, a 10-metre matchstick, and even the odd penguin in the glittering waters off Circular Quay.

Coming of age

Much has been made in the global media of Sydney's new-found maturity in the wake of its universal Olympic adulation. Ask a Sydneysider about the city, however, and they will probably tell you that the things that make Sydney great haven't really changed. It may no longer be young, but it doesn't especially want to grow old.

At a glance

Circular Quay and The Rocks

In the shadow of the Central Business District (CBD), Circular Quay is the epicentre of tourist activity within the inner city. Flanked by the Harbour Bridge and The Rocks on one side and the conspicuous Opera House on the other, and yet collectively and almost disconcertingly all within waving distance across the bustling harbour to the North Shore, it is one of the most stunning locations in Australia. For the visitor it is a place to satisfy all the expectations of scale, a place to bombard the senses, to be entertained by (or run a mile from) street performers, or to depart by ferry or train to a whole host of other attractions. The Rocks deserves equal celebration. A historic enclave that for decades was the notorious hub of the emerging colony, it has, after considerable renovation since the 1960s, become a major tourist attraction in itself.

City Centre: the CBD

Many visitors find the city centre, the modern and corporate face of Sydney, a chaotic place. It is chilled by modern high rises and disturbed by the collective din of corporate Australia. Yet despite that it is still worth taking the plunge and joining the purposeful floods of humanity through its gargantuan corridors to discover its hidden gems. Most notable are the scattered historic buildings that, though dwarfed by the mighty, have survived and stood up to the city's ceaseless modern development.

Darling Harbour and Chinatown

Created with much aplomb to celebrate Sydney's Bicentennial in 1988, Darling Harbour has been revitalized to such an extent and with so much success, that even the waves seem to clap with appreciation. Here, day and night, ferries and jetcats (Sydney's high-speed catamarans) bring hordes of visitors to marvel at its modern architecture and its high-profile aquatically themed attractions, or to revel in its casino and trendy waterside bars and restaurants. Framed beautifully against a backdrop of the glistening CBD, it is intricately colourful, urban and angular – right down to the last ripple of each landscaped fountain. The western fringe of Darling Harbour heralds the start of Chinatown, perhaps the city's most notable living monument to its cosmopolitan populous.

City West: Glebe to Parramatta

Separated by Sydney University (which adds spice) and situated just to the west of Darling Harbour, the enclaves of Glebe and Newtown are renowned for their exotic and bizarre range of shops and their eclectic, cosmopolitan cafés and restaurants. Nearby Leichhardt possesses a particular mediterranean appeal and has been dubbed Sydney's 'Little Italy'. To the north the once seedy suburb of Balmain has seen a makeover in recent years with a desire to join the party. Further west are the contrasting attractions of the Homebush Olympic Park and the historic 'town within the city' – Parramatta. While the soils of Homebush sprouted some of the nation's finest modern architecture in order to stage the 2000 Olympic Games, it was the soils of Parramatta that saved the wretched souls of the First Fleet facing starvation in Port Jackson in 1790.

City East: Kings Cross to Bondi

Neatly divided from the CBD by the leafy avenues and grandiose attractions in and around Hyde Park and the Domain are the inner-city suburbs of Woolloomooloo, Potts Point Darlinghurst, Surry Hills and King's Cross – Sydney's 'nightlife capital', somewhat overrated and facing stiff competition. Fringing 'The Cross', Darlinghurst, Potts Point and Woolloomooloo are all blessed with some fine restaurants, cafés and pubs, while Oxford Street provides the focus and social epicentre of Sydney's famously overt gay community and the main venue for the annual Sydney Mardis Gras. Further east Oxford Street then fringes Paddington, one of Sydney's most attractive suburbs: a place where quiet, leafy streets lined with tiny Victorian terrace houses possess an elfinesque appeal, yet at the same time a giant price tag. Beyond Paddington land gives way to ocean and the popular and laid-back beachside suburbs of Bondi, Bronte and Coogee. Australia's most famous swathe of sand, Bondi, with its scantily clad, sickeningly tanned sun worshippers and stalwart Sydney surf set needs little introduction but the lesser-known beaches fronting Bronte and Coogee are almost equally appealing.

City North: Manly to the Northern Beaches

North of the harbour Sydney's 'other half' stretches all the way to the boundaries of the Ku-ring-gai National Park. The big attraction are the northern beaches, with Manly, near the Sydney harbour entrance, a self-contained beachside resort providing the perfect day trip from the city centre. Fringing the harbour inland lies some of the city's most sought-after real estate nestled in the pretty and well-heeled suburbs of Mosman, Balmoral and Cremorne.

Walkabout

Further west, beyond the unremarkable and uncelebrated western suburbs (Sydney's poorest communities), are the majestic Blue Mountains, one of Australia's largest and most beautiful national parks. To the north of the city the Hawkesbury River Region has less precipitous rural scenery and Ku-ring-gai Chase National Park adds Aboriginal rock art to sandstone and bush walks. To the south, the Royal National Park, Australia's oldest, is fringed by beautiful beaches, while Botany Bay National Park, bordering the fringes of the city, is the historic site of captain Cooks first landing in April 1770.

★ **Ten of the best**

Best

1 **Circular Quay** The vista and the buzz of activity, with the Opera House, the Harbour Bridge and the harbour itself, are the epitome of Sydney's character, p41.

2 **Taronga Zoo** Take the ferry to meet some of Australia's remarkable species at the 'zoo with the view', p89.

3 **Bondi Beach** Don your trendiest beachwear and join the beautiful people, p85.

4 **Botanical Gardens** Escape the city buzz with a short stroll. Meet the resident bat colony then emerge to enjoy one of the best views of the Opera House from Macquarie Point, p59.

5 **North Head** and **Manly** Take the classic ferry ride to Manly from Circular Quay. Spend a day at the beach, or hire a bike and cycle to North Head for more stunning views, p91.

6 **The Australian Museum** Cool off within its hallowed walls and stretch your mind beyond the bounds of the great modern city across this vast and truly remarkable land, p59.

7 **Queen Victoria Building** Indulge in some world-class retail therapy, amidst old and new, at one of the city's most remarkably renovated historic buildings, p56.

8 **Sydney Fish Market** Join an early morning tour, taking a close look at the array of sea creatures from thumb-sized octopuses to man-sized tuna, p66.

9 **Kings St, Newtown** People-watch in a cosmopolitan restaurant, or wander through shops selling everything from secondhand books to black leather codpieces, p152.

10 **Balmoral Beach** Join the locals for an early morning dip on one of the north shore's best beaches, p90

Trip planner

Sydney is a year-round destination attracting over two million international visitors annually. Summer (October to March) is generally considered the 'high season', but in reality accommodation availability, costs and city services tend to oscillate according to the vagaries of major city events, especially high-profile extravaganzas like the Mardi Gras, or the sporting 'majors' like cricket and rugby (union and league) finals or tests (see Festivals and events, p185).

The weather in Sydney is generally pleasant and warm year round and you will find it unusual to have to don a pair of long trousers, a jumper or a pair of sensible shoes. But that does not mean its coastal position offers constant protection from Australia's meteorological extremes. Uncomfortable heat, dramatic storms and even hailstones the size of golf balls all feature, with summer offering the worst. Winter can also see a few rainy days, though hardly a European number.

A long weekend

Day one For sunrise get yourself (and your camera) in position at Macquarie Point (harbourside) and the Royal Botanical Gardens which offers one of the best views of the Opera House and the harbour bridge. Then head for the Opera House via the waterfront, taking a short diversion in to the heart of the botanical gardens to see the aromatic bat colony (see p59). At the Opera House lose yourself in creative photography or simple awe amidst its shell-like structure and its views across to the bridge. From there, take your time negotiating Circular Quay (see p41) perhaps stopping for a leisurely breakfast below the concourse, or along Opera Quays. Then, make your way to The Rocks via Campbell's Cove, where the replica of the *Bounty* is moored and where you are presented with more stunning views back over the Opera House. Continue round to Dawes Point Park and marvel at the sheer size of the harbour bridge. Other great views are available by climbing the southeast tower (access off Cumberland St). From there, head back towards The Rocks and down George Street (which hosts the bustling Rocks market at the weekend). Sample the many sights and sounds of the rocks and perhaps book a 'Bridgeclimb' for the following day (see p48). For lunch, (perhaps a croc or roo steak) get a pavement table at the *Australian Hotel* (see p147).

In the afternoon, catch a ferry from Circular Quay to Taronga Zoo, (see p89) or for the soporific, head for Balmoral Beach. Better still, get naked with the locals at the little-known naturist beach Cobblers Beach (see p90). In the evening, return to The Rocks or Darling Harbour and cruise the menus for dinner.

Day two Around the following put aside some time for your 'BridgeClimb'. Again, start early with a fascinating tour of Sydney Fish Market (see p66). From there, keeping the wallet firmly closed, head via the Casino to the National Maritime Museum (see p63). Be sure to take the submarine tour then cross the Pyrmont Bridge to the Sydney Aquarium (see p62). In the afternoon, (preferably on a Sunday) head for Circular Quay and catch the ferry to Watson's Bay. Sample the seafood delights of *Doyle's* on the Beach, or join the fray next door at the al fresco *Watson's Bay Hotel* (see p160).

Enjoy a leisurely walk to South Head ignoring the barefaced cheek of Lady Bay naturist beach (see p84). Hit Darlinghurst for dinner and perhaps Kings Cross for an eventful night on the town (see p173). Alternatively try Chinatown and a less riotous night out around Darling Harbour (see p172).

Day three Time to relax. Depending on the hangover, either drive to North Head (via Manly) at dawn for the memorable views across the city, or take a more leisurely trip later in the morning by ferry to Manly from Circular Quay. In Manly, spend the best part of the day on the beach, try body boarding or take a surf lesson (see p208).

If you are feeling more adventurous head north to see Palm Beach and enjoy the views with a short walk to the Barrenjoey

Lighthouse (see p96). Alternatively, spend a leisurely breakfast at the beachside cafés at Bronte (see p160). Then take the coastal path to Bondi spending the rest of the day on the world-famous beach.

In the evening see if you can secure a last-minute booking for a performance at the Opera House, or see what else is on offer at other city theatres. If that does not appeal perhaps try your luck at the Casino (see p180).

As unlikely as it is, if your long weekend is interrupted with inclement weather take in the Australian Museum (see p59), or the Powerhouse Museum (see p68), or shop in the Queen Victoria Building and the CBD (see p193).

One to three weeks

The above will keep you blissfully occupied for at least three days and given more time you can stretch it out with copious amounts of sunbathing, shopping or further sightseeing. Within the confines of the city other attractions and activities to consider are harbour cruises; a fine option being the trip to Olympic Park or a luncheon trip aboard the replica of The *Bounty* (see p151).

Then you may consider other city centre sights like the Art Gallery of New South Wales (see p61) or the noteworthy Brett Whitley Museum and Gallery (see p82). Take to a canoe to experience a more intimate exploration of the harbour (see p208), or get close up and personal with a koala or a frogmouth at the Featherdale Wildlife Park (see p77).

Further afield at least a day in the Blue Mountains is highly recommended (see p101), while other options for walks, camping and swimming include Ku-ring-gai Chase (see p114), Botany Bay (see p117) or the Royal National Parks (see p115), all less than an hour from the city.

Contemporary Sydney

After a century in the grips of infant dependence, and another finding its way through teenage confusion, Sydney has successfully shaken off its convict shackles, together with its colonial past, and is well on the way to maturity. The country's largest and most popular metropolis is leading the way in the development of Australia's very own enviable identity, but, like any city, it is not without its issues and its problems, both social and – given its geographical position on the very fringe of the world's driest continent – natural.

True to its foundation, Sydney has developed into one of the most cosmopolitan cities in the world. For a former penal colony that used to hang you for pocketing a potato, it is now (at least on the surface) the very embodiment of an emancipated society. Where riots and alleged police brutality were once the reaction to the inaugural Gay and Lesbian Mardis Gras in 1978, you now have a world-famous annual event lauded as one of the most colourful in Australia. And one indeed in which the police now have their very own float and must keep a firm grip on their handcuffs as well as their truncheons.

A variety of nationalities thrive, adding their own style and charisma to distinct suburban enclaves including the long-established Chinatown, Leichhardt's 'Little Italy' and Lakemba's growing Lebanese community. Superficially, for local gourmands and tourists, this smorgasbord of nationalities offers a plethora of restaurants serving up an eclectic mix of Modern Australian dishes garnished with inordinate global influences. But beyond the stomachs and menus, this social content also creates rumblings of social disharmony. With the sparkling harbour and famous city center awash with stunning icons and visitor attractions it is all too easy to ignore the fact that beyond the inner city there exist fragmented suburbs and communities that never had the same opportunity to feel the warmth of the Olympic flame

Sea and commerce
The buildings of Sydney's gleaming Central Business District rise high behind the waters of the Harbour and boats old and new.

or to share in the financial, social and aesthetic benefits afforded to the city centre. Like the nether regions of most modern metropolises it is here in the stigmatized and largely unvisited outer suburbs, like Liverpool or Bankstown, where you will find elevated crime and unemployment rates and the worst of the city's social deprivation and racism. Over the years various attempts have been made by both local and federal government to address these social issues but perhaps because of the complexity of the problems, all too often these have had limited success. With the population of the city increasing by almost 100 people daily, it seems the problems will probably get worse before they get better.

One range of issues that continues to gnaw away at the city's very social fabric are centered round Aboriginal rights and their often troubled social integration. The majority of Sydneysiders are not aware that the city has the largest Aboriginal population in Australia. Certainly, beyond the odd Aboriginal didgeridoo player busking at Circular Quay, you would never guess it from the city centre. It seems in glitzy, sexy Sydney, social problems are largely out of sight, out of mind.

Also in recent months with the 11 September terrorist attacks in 2001 and the tragic Bali bombings in October 2002 (which took over 90 Australian lives, many from Sydney), prejudice towards the city's Muslim communities is on the increase.

Of added concern to Australians generally is the highly discomforting prospect that their showpiece city may actually become a global terrorist target. It seems Prime Minister John Howard's highly contentious comments in November 2002, in which he hinted that the current Australian government might join the US in using pre-emptive strikes as a deterrent to terrorism in the region, have only added fuel to the fire. For a city so famous for its laid-back attitudes it seems the great wave of global paranoia has arrived. For Sydneysiders especially, this will take some getting used to.

Human threats and social issues aside, in the urban jungle of coastal Sydney, it is also easy to forget or ignore the vast, arid continent on its doorstep. Yet, with a vengeance and in various forms, Mother Nature still comes calling both uninvited and unwelcome. In 1999, what seemed like just another entertaining storm turned violent when a blitzkrieg of hailstones, some the size of golf balls, rained down on the city causing over one billion dollars worth of damage.

Of far more concern and with increasing recurrence are another age-old natural phenomenon: bush fires. Almost annually for over a decade fires have ravaged the surrounding national parks and the fringes of the city, destroying numerous properties, costing hundreds of millions of dollars, taking several lives and muting Sydney's vivid colours with a cloak of grey, acrid smoke. A recent drought throughout New South Wales has only added to the problem prompting the federal government to offer $360 million dollars in what has been dubbed 'Exceptional Circumstances Drought Assistance'.

Tourism is the fuel that drives the city, or at the very least the oil in its engine. As the principal gateway to the continent and with over two million international visitors each year, it is perhaps inevitable and remains on the increase. Although the city's assets were never a great secret, the 2000 Olympic Games and the subsequent declaration of Olympics Committee President, Juan Samaranch that they were the 'best ever' only enhanced this image. With record-breaking amounts of money spent on inner-city rejuvenation, improved infrastructure and some of the most modern sporting venues on the planet, it set the stage for Sydney to show off its wares and its deep love affair with the sporting lifestyle. More importantly for Australians, it was yet another opportunity to prove their mighty sporting talent and world dominance beyond the traditional rugby union and cricket. It is, after all, Sydney's very own human version of a harbour ferry –

Ian Thorpe (nicknamed the 'Thorpedo') – who proved in no uncertain terms that swimming should be added to the list. Then, on terra firma, and with much smaller feet, there were others, like 400 m runner Kathy Freeman, who showed with unflappable determination that despite the contentious issues surrounding Aboriginals, their flag could be held aloft in front of over 100,000 mainly white Australians with just as much credence and celebration as any other.

Although exceptionally strong at sport, some argue that Sydney consistently loses much of its cultural talent overseas. It is however enjoying something of a resurgence in recent years, especially in the medium of film.

Hi-tech blockbusters, starring some of Hollywood's most celebrated actors, like *Matrix II* (Keanu Reeves), *Mission Impossible II* (Tom Cruise) and the new *Star Wars* trilogy were all filmed or partly filmed in Sydney and compete with the home-grown talents and successes of Australia's very own stars like Nicole Kidman, Mel Gibson, Cate Blanchett and Guy Pearce (Russell Crowe, star of *Gladiator* and *A Beautiful Mind*, was actually born in New Zealand).

So what of the future for Sydney, this brash, young city with an exuberance and outlook that reflects its tender age, a city that yearns so much for independence, that defies nature and yet, beneath the facade, is dependent on the moist coastal climate?

Will natural bush fires continue to tear chunks from the fringes of the city and human social issues continue to trouble its people? Will terrorism one day strike at Sydney's very heart? These questions are impossible to answer. What is sure is that although on the surface she is almost sickeningly beautiful, vain, a show off, a material girl and behind the facade has some deep-seated problems, Sydney is also genuinely happy, friendly and always great company.

Travel essentials

For those visiting Sydney briefly on board a luxury cruise liner, Circular Quay offers a truly memorable introduction, but the vast majority of travellers inevitably arrive in less salubrious fashion both bleary-eyed and jet-lagged, at Sydney's Kingsford Smith Airport. Transportation to the city centre from both international and domestic terminals is readily available. By rail or coach, Central Station and the principal coach terminal are located side by side just south of the Central Business District. Public transport in Sydney is efficient and convenient: these days you can negotiate the city and see the major sights on just about every form of transportation known to mankind. You have a choice of ferry, car, bus, rail, or mono-rail, though the old traditional method – by foot, still remains a realistic and lively way to get around the city centre. And you may find yourself on the water as much as land; the great hub of public transportation in the city centre revolves around Circular Quay, which sits like the doorstep to a huge termite hill at the base of the CBD.

Getting there

Air

From UK and Europe The main route, and the cheapest, is via Asia, though fares will also be quoted via North America or Africa. The Asia route usually takes from 20 to 30 hours including stops. There are no non-stop routes, so it's worth checking out what stopovers are on offer: this might be your only chance to see Kuala Lumpur. Stopovers of a few nights do not usually increase the cost of the ticket appreciably. The cheapest return flights to Sydney, off-season, will be around £500 (€789). Stand-by prices rise to at least £800 (€1,263) around Christmas.

From New Zealand There are direct **Qantas** flights from Auckland, Christchurch and Wellington to Sydney. **Air New Zealand**, and **Freedom Air** are the other two main carriers, both offering routes that **Qantas** do not. Expect to pay a minimum of NZ$500 for a return to Sydney.

From the Americas There are direct **Qantas** flights from Los Angeles, Vancouver and New York to Sydney. The cost of a standard return in the high season from starts from around US$2,200 from Vancouver, US$2,000 from New York, and US$1,700 from Los Angeles. There are also direct flights from Buenos Aires to Sydney. Other airlines flying from North America include **Air New Zealand**, **Air Canada**, and **Singapore Airlines**.

Round-the-World Round-the-World (RTW) tickets can be a real bargain if you stick to the most popular routes, sometimes working out even cheaper than a return fare. RTWs start at around £750 (€1,200) or US$1,500, depending on the season. Sydney is easy to include on a RTW itinerary.

Airlines and travel agents

Air Canada, T 9232 5222, www.aircanada.ca
Air New Zealand, T 13 2476, www.airnz.co.uk
British Airways, T 1300 767 177, www.ba.com
Emirates, T 03 9940 7807, www.emirates.com
Freedom Air, T 1800 122 223, www.freedom.co.nz
Qantas, T 131313, www.qantas.com
Singapore Airlines, T 9350 0100, www.singaporeair.com
Air Brokers International, (USA) T 800 8833273,
www.airbrokers.com
Council Travel, (USA) T 800 COUNCIL,
www.destinations-group.com
Ebookers, www.ebookers.com
Expedia, T 0870-0500808 (UK), www.expedia.com
STA Travel, T 0870-1600599 (UK), www.statravel.com
Trailfinders, T 020-79371234 (UK), www.trailfinders.co.uk
Travelocity, www.travelocity.com

Airport information Sydney's **Kingsford Smith Airport** is located 9 km south of the city centre. Given a major overhaul for the 2000 Olympic Games, its negotiation is pretty straightforward and the facilities are excellent. There is a Tourism New South Wales information desk in the main arrivals concourse where help is at hand to organize transport, accommodation bookings and flight arrival information, **T** 9667 6065, www.sydneyairport.com Additionally, The Sydney Airport Help Desk is located in the centre of the terminal (Departures). Volunteer **Airport Ambassadors** (identified by gold jackets) are also on hand to answer any questions. Other airport facilities include cash ATM's, Thomas Cook and Travelex Foreign Exchange, car hire, a post office and even a medical centre. Unfortunately due to the threat of terrorist attacks the locker service at Sydney Airport International Terminal is currently unavailable. The airport is open from 0400-2300 daily. Sydney's Domestic Terminal is a short distance west of the International Terminal and has also been fully modernized. Public transport from the airport to the city centre (and between terminals) is readily available within a short walk of both terminal buildings. The green and yellow **Airport Express**, T 131500, services the city centre (daily 0500-2300) including the Central Railway Station, Circular Quay and Wynyard bus and principal rail stations (bus 300, $7, child $3.50, return $12, tickets from the driver) with connecting services to Kings Cross, Bondi, Coogee (bus 350) and Darling Harbour, Glebe (bus 352). There is a ticket booth in the main bus area. **Taxis** are readily available outside the terminal (south). A trip to the city centre takes about 30 minutes and costs about $25. There is also a new **rail link** between the main city stations to the Domestic Terminal every 10-15 minutes, daily from 0500-2400, from $10 one-way (20 minutes).

Bus

The **Sydney Coach Terminal** is located in the Central Railway Station, T 9212 3433, 0600-2230 daily. A left luggage facility and showers are available in the terminal. **Greyhound Pioneer**, T 132030, and **Premier Motor Service**, T 133410, are the three main interstate and state coach companies offering regular daily schedules to most main centres. **Firefly Express**, 482 Pitt St, T 1300 730 740 / T 9211 1644, www.fireflyexpress.com.au operate a daily/ overnight Melbourne to Sydney, or Sydney to Melbourne service and drop off/pick up at their 482 Pitt St terminal. **Murray's**, T 132259, offer a *Canberra Express* service three times daily from the main coach terminal on Eddy Avenue.

Train

All interstate and New South Wales (NSW) State destination trains also arrive and depart from Sydney's Central **Railway Station** on Eddy Avenue. There is an information booth and ticket offices on the main platform concourse. **Countrylink** are the main interstate operators operating with a combination of coach and rail to all the main interstate and NSW destinations, **T** 132232 (daily 0630-2200), bookings@countrylink.nsw.gov.au   There is a Countrylink Travel Centre located at central station, **T** 9955 4237, while Town Hall Station, **T** 9379 4076, Wynyard Station, **T** 9224 4744, Circular Quay, **T** 9224 3400 and Bondi Junction **T** 937-9377, all have on the spot **CityRail** information booths.

First class and economy fares vary so you are advised to shop around and compare prices with the various coach operators. Ask about their *Backtracker Pass* which offers unlimited journeys on entire rail and coach network, including Brisbane, 14 days $165-6 months $330. The *East Coast Discovery Pass* gives you six months economy class travel, one way, either north or south with unlimited stopovers; Melbourne $93.50; Cairns $247.50. The railway station also houses the main interstate city coach terminal (**McCaffertys** and **Greyhound**) and from there or Pitt Street and George Street you can pick up regular city and suburban buses. The **Airport Express** also stops outside the train station (coach terminal). For information **T** 131500, www.sydneytransport.net.au **Great Southern Rail**, **T** 132147, www.gsr.com.au operate services from Sydney to Perth (*Indian Pacific*) via Broken Hill and Adelaide and Sydney to Alice Springs (*The Ghan*) via Melbourne and Adelaide. **Countrylink** operate the *XPT* (11 hours, twice daily, one overnight) between Sydney and Melbourne and daily to Brisbane.

Getting around

Car

Travelling by car around Sydney is a nightmare with numerous tolls, expensive parking and omnipresent parking wardens to add to your woes. There really is no need to see the sights by car but if you must take lots of change both in coinage and underwear. For car rental companies see Directory, p223. The **National Roads**

and Motorists' Association (NRMA) is based at 74-76 King Street, CBD, **T** 132132.

Train

Sydney's excellent 24-hour double-decker train services are a convenient way to reach the city centre and outlying areas, or to link in with bus and ferry services. Much of the CBD line is underground. Fares are generally quite cheap and start at $1. Savings of up to 40% can be made with 'Off-Peak Tickets' which operate after 0900 on weekdays. Further savings can be made with the *TravelPass* and *Sydney Pass* system (see box, p30).

There are numerous 'coloured' routes with the green or purple **City Circle** (Central, Town Hall, Wynyard, Circular Quay, St James and the Museum) and blue **Eastern Suburbs Line** (Central, Town Hall, Martin Place, Kings Cross, Edgecliff, Bondi Junction) being the most convenient for visitors. Tickets and detailed information is available at all major stations. For information about suburban trains in Sydney, **T** 131500, www.131500.com.au

For information about all public transport in Sydney, **T** 131500. (daily 0600-2200) Prior to arrival it is well worth having a look at the website www.131500.com.au If you intend to be in the city for a while, the free *Sydney Public Transport Directory* is useful, available from the Sydney VIC.

Bus

Note that the usually very congenial drivers do not automatically stop at bus stops so if you are alone you must signal the driver, or at night gesticulate wildly. The **STA** (Sydney Buses) are the principal operators with the standard buses being blue and white, the **Airport Express** (a very Aussie green and yellow), the **Sydney Explorer** (red) and the **Bondi Explorer** (blue). Standard bus fares

! Children usually travel half-price on public transport and there are also family concessions on most fares.

Visas

Visas are subject to change, so check first with your local Australian Embassy or High Commission. All travellers to Australia, except New Zealand citizens, must have a valid visa to enter Australia. These must be arranged prior to travel (allow two months) and cannot be organized at Australian airports. **Tourist visas**, which are free, are available from your local Australian Embassy or High Commission, or in some countries, in electronic format (an **Electronic Travel Authority** or ETA) from their websites, and from selected travel agents and airlines. The **Working Holiday Visa**, which must also be arranged prior to departure, is available to people between 18 and 30 from certain countries that have reciprocal arrangements with Australia. It allows multiple entry for one year from first arrival. See www.immi.gov.au/visitors for further information.

start at $1.50-4.70 depending on distance and subsequent zone. If you intend to travel regularly by bus a *Travel Ten* ticket is recommended ($11-$39) while further savings can be also be made with the *TravelPass* and *Sydney Pass* system. (see box, p30.)

The **Explorer** buses cost $30 for the full return trip ($50 for two days). There is an on-board commentary and you can hop on and off at will. Both leave at regular intervals from Circular Quay. For all of the above bus fares children travel half-price and there are also family concessions. Most *Explorer* buses operate between 0840 and 1722 only The local (green) *Olympic Explorer* offers trips around the Homebush Bay site and links with ferry services from Circular Quay ($20 with ferry, $10 without), while the weekend (blue and yellow) *Parramatta Explorer* leaves every 20 minutes from the RiverCat ferry terminal in Parramatta, $10 (ex Rivercat). For information about suburban buses in Sydney, **T** 131500, www.131500.com.au

Ferry

A trip on one of Sydney's ageing, almost iconic green and gold harbour ferries is a wonderful experience and an ideal way to see the city, as well as reach many of the major attractions and suburbs. A short return voyage from the busy Circular Quay terminal to the zoo, Mosman or Cremorne on the North Shore, during both day and night is highly recommended. The principal operator is **Sydney Ferries** that run the 'green and golds' and also the fast JetCats to Manly and RiverCat to Homebush Bay/Parramatta. Several independent companies also operate out of Circular Quay offering a wide range of cruises as well as suburban transportation and water taxis. **Hegarty's Ferries**, T 9206 1167, operates daily services from Circular Quay to Milson's Point, Lavender Bay, McMahon's Point, Jeffrey Street and Beulah Street. **Matilda**, T 9264 7377, offer a range of cruise options and *The Rocket* to Darling Harbour/Lane Cove. For water-taxi services see Taxi, below.

Like the buses ferry fares are priced according to zone and start at a single trip for $4.20. A *Daytripper Pass* (one day) costs $13.40. If you intend to travel regularly by ferry a *FerryTen* ticket (from $26.50) is recommended, while further savings can be also be made with the *TravelPass* and *Sydney Pass* system, (see box, p30.)

Various travel/entry combo tickets are offered to the major harbourside sights including Taronga Zoo, see p89, and the Sydney Aquarium, see p62. Various Cruises are also on offer throughout the day and the evening.

For ferry information **T** 131500, www.sydneytransport.com.au The main Sydney Ferries Information Centre can be found opposite Wharf 4, Circular Quay.

Metro MonoRail and LightRail

Opened in July 1988, as a gift to Sydney in celebration of Australia's Bicentennial, the **MonoRail** runs in a loop around

Travel and sightseeing passes

There are numerous, popular travel pass systems in operation in Sydney. The *DayTripper Pass* gives all day access to Sydney's trains, bus and ferries within the suburban area from $13.40, child $6.70. Tickets can be purchased at any rail, bus or ferry sales or information outlet, or on the buses themselves. *TravelPass* allows unlimited, weekly, quarterly or yearly combined travel throughout designated zones or sections. A seven-day pass for example, covering the inner (orange) zone costs $34, child $17.50.

For the tourist staying only a few days the best bet is the *Sydney Pass* which offers unlimited travel on ferry and standard buses as well as the *Sydney* and *Bondi Explorer* routes and the four *STA Harbour Cruises*. They are sold as a 3-day ($90, child $45), 5-day ($120, child $60) or 7-day ($140, child $70) Return. *Airport Express* transfers are also included and family conssesions apply. Note that discount, ten-trip *TravelTen* (bus) and *FerryTen* passes are also available from $11.

The *SeeSydneyCard* gives unlimited admission to a wide variety of attractions, activities and tours, and offers reductions at some restaurants and shops. The card also includes optional public transport. Adult cards range from one-day for $49 (with transport included $62) to a week at $149 ($207) and children one-day $29 (with transport $35.50) to a week at $89 ($118). For more information and purchasing contact the major VICs or call T 92551788, www.seesydneycard.com

If you have a specific interest in museums and historical buildings you might also consider the *Ticket Through Time* (valid for three months) that combines many of the major attractions administered by the *Historic Houses Trust*. $23, children $10, family $40. Ask the VIC for details and a leaflet.

Darling Harbour and South Western CBD and provides as much of a novelty journey as a convenient way of getting from A to B. Even if you never use it you will doubtless see it as it slips gently past above your head like a legless metal centipede. The carriages run every three to five minutes, Monday-Thursday 0700-2200, Friday and Saturday 0700-2400 and Sunday 0800-2200. The standard fare (one loop) is $4 while a *Day Pass* costs $8. Children under five travel free and discounts are available to some major attractions.

The new *LightRail* network is Sydney's newest transport system linking Central Station with Lilyfield, via a number of stops within the South West CBD and Darling Harbour, as well as the Casino, Fish Market and Glebe. It is a 24-hour service with trains every 10-15 minutes from 0600-2400 and every 30 minutes 2400-0600. There are two fare zones starting at a single journey at $2.60. A *Day Pass* with unlimited stops costs $8. For information, **T** 9285 5600, www.metromonorail.com.au

Land and Water Taxi

Sydney's taxi service, once of rather dubious quality, was given a major revamp for the 2000 Olympics and it is now much improved. Ranks are located near every railway station, at Circular Quay and numerous spots in the CBD, otherwise hail one as required. From 2200-0600 higher tariffs apply. The minimum (hailed) flagfall is $2.20 with about a $1.10 charge per kilometre thereafter. On short journeys tipping is not expected. There are several companies including **Combined**, **T** 8332 8888, ABC **T** 132522, **Premie**r, **T** 131017, **Legion**, **T** 131451 and **RSL**, **T** 132211. Water taxis operate all over the harbour with most being based on the western edge of Circular Quay. The main operators are **Taxis Afloat**, **T** 9955 3222, **Harbour Shuttle**, **T** 9810 5010 and **Water Taxis Combined**, **T** 9555 8888.

Bicycle

Unless you are a courier with a death wish and want to do repeated impersonations of Garfield on the exterior of city buses, travel by bike within the city centre is not recommended. The suburbs however are a little less manic, but then you always risk returning to find only a bell and a padlock. Several companies offer bike hire from about $30 per day or $170 per week, see Directory, p223.

Blue Mountains

Although public transport to and around the Blue Mountains is generally good, hiring a car (see p223) allows you to make the most of the numerous viewpoints and sights within the region. The route through the Blue Mountains is generally easily negotiable. From Sydney, take the M4 ($2 toll), eventually crossing the **Neapean River**, before it forms the **Great Western Highway** at **Glenbrook** (65 km). Then, beginning the ascent of the main plateau and following the same route as the railway line, you pass through Blaxland, Springwood, Faulconbridge and Woodford, before arriving at **Wentworth Falls**. It is in Wentworth that you reach the top of the main plateau at an average height of just above 1,000 m. From Wentworth Falls the road continues west through the northern edges of **Leura** and **Katoomba**, then north, through the heart of **Blackheath** and **Mount Victoria**. From Mount Victoria you then begin the descent to **Lithgow** (154 km). The rather peculiarly named **Bells Line of Road** provides another access point across the mountains from **Windsor** on the east to Mount Victoria on the Great Western Hwy (77 km).

The best way to arrive independently is by **train**. They leave Sydney's Central Station (**Countrylink** and/or **CityLink** Platforms) on the hour, daily, well in to the evening, stopping at all major towns through the Blue Mountains to Mount Victoria and beyond, **T** 132232/**T** 131500. The journey to Katoomba takes about two hours and costs around $15 day-return. **CityRail**, **T** 131500, in conjunction with **Fantastic Aussie Tours**, **T** 1300 300 915, also offer a number of rail/coach tour options with **Blue MountainsLink** operating Monday to Friday and **Blue Mountains ExplorerLink** operating daily. The price includes return transport and a tour on arrival in Katoomba.

Greyhound, (**T** 132030, offer standard daily **coach** transportation on the westbound run to Dubbo. Numerous **coach** companies also offer day sightseeing tours from Sydney. Most of the buses leave from Circular Quay. **Aerocity Shuttles**, **T** 4782 1866, offer direct links from Sydney Airport.

Hawkesbury River region
There is no public transport to Wisemans Ferry or St Albans. By road, from central Sydney, take the Pacific Hwy (Hwy 1) northeast to Hornsby. Just beyond Hornsby take a left on to Galston Road to join the Northern Road (Hwy 36). Gradually you will leave the shackles of urbanity behind and begin to reach scenic countryside through Glenorie and Maroota prior to sighting the magnificent Hawkesbury River at Wisemans Ferry (97 km).

Ku-ring-gai Chase National Park
By **car** access is via Bobbin Head Road, via the Pacific Highway (from the south) or from Ku-ring-gai Chase Road via F3 Freeway (from the north). Access to the eastern side (West Head Road and West Head Lookout) is from Mona Vale Road, Northern Beaches. The nearest public transport (western side) by **train** is with **CityRail**, **T** 131500 (Northern Line) from Central Station to Berowa, Mount Ku-ring-gai and Mount Colah, then walk to Bobbin Head (3-6 km). A better alternative is to catch a **bus** (L90) to Palm Beach (eastern side) then a **ferry** to Basin Beach. Ferry Cruises also run to Bobbin Head (see Northern Beaches). Vehicle entry costs $10 per day.

Royal National Park
By **car** from Sydney take the Princes Hwy south and follow signs for Audley (left, at Loftus on Farnell Avenue and McKell Avenue).

Overground
Sydney's monorail zips around Darling Harbour every few minutes, on stilts above street level.

By **train** take **CityRail**, **T** 131500 (Illawarra line) from Central Station to Loftus (4 km from Audley), Engadine, Heathcote, Waterfall or Otford. You can also alight at Cronulla and take the short crossing by **ferry** to Bundeena at the park's northeastern corner, **T** 9523 2990, from $3. Vehicle entry costs $10 per day.

Botany Bay National Park
Access to the northern sector is via Anzac Parade. Sydney Buses, **T** 131500, offer regular daily **bus** services from Railway Square (number 393) or Circular Quay (394) in Sydney's CBD. To get to the southern sector by **car**, follow the Princes Hwy south, take a left onto The Boulevard, and then follow Captain Cook Drive. By **train** from Sydney's Central Station, take **CityRail** (**T** 131500) to Cronulla (Illawarra line), then **Kurnell Bus** (number 987, **T** 9523 4047) to the park gates. Vehicle entry to the park costs $6.

Tours

Aboriginal Discoveries is an Aboriginal owned and operated outfit that offer day, half-day and one-and-a-half-hour guided tours and cruises covering some of Sydney's most significant pre-European, Aboriginal sites. **T** 9568 6880. A tour explaining the significance to original Aboriginal population of the area now covered by the *Royal Botanical Gardens* can also be done (see p60). For more botanical tours of the gardens see p60.

The best way to see The Rocks properly is to join the official **Rocks Walking Tour**, which is an entertaining and informative insight in to both past and present. Bookings can be made at the Sydney VIC, 106 George Street or at the Walks Office, Shop K4, Kendall Lane. The tours take an hour and a half, departing at 1030,1230 and 1430 weekdays and 1130 and 1400 weekends, $17.50, children $10.50, family $45.55, **T** 9247 6678, bookings recommended.

For **Harbour Cruises** see box, p64. For tours of several **Harbour Islands** see p50 and for tours of the **Sydney Opera House** see p41.

Tourist information

Beyond the Visitor Information booth at the airport International Arrivals Terminal, the first stop for any visitor should be the **Sydney Visitor Centre (**106 George Street, The Rocks, **T** 9255 1788, (**T** 1800 067 676 free from outside Sydney and within Australia) **F** 9241 5010, www.sydneyvisitorcentre.com *daily 0900-1800, Map 2, C5, p248*) In a smart 1864 former sailors' home, the centre provides a comprehensive service, which includes information, brochures, maps and reservations for hotels, tours, cruises, restaurants and other city based activities. The centre can book stand-by accommodation (discounted rates), but this is a face-to-face service only. Alternatively visitors can contact some hotels and tour/activity operators via the free-to-use phones.

There is another principal VIC at **Darling Harbour**, south end of Cockle Bay, next door to IMAX, **T** 19022 60568, www.darlingharbour.com.au *Daily 1000-1800*. It offers much the same in services as The Rocks' centre but has an emphasis on sights and activities within Darling Harbour itself. Neither centre issues public transport tickets. Small manned information booths are located at the corner of Pitt Street and Alfred Street, Circular Quay; opposite Street Andrews Cathedral near the Town Hall on George Street and on Martin Place, near Elizabeth Street.

There are several independent travel offices designed mainly to cater for backpackers including **Travellers Contact Point**, 7th Floor, 428 George Street, **T** 9221 8744, www.travellers.com.au *Mon-Fri 0900-1800, Sat 1000-1600*, which also offers mail forwarding and employment advice. Most of these offices also have internet facilities. The **Australian Travel Specialists** cater for the full range of traveller and have offices throughout the city, including one at Wharf 6, Circular Quay, **T** 9555 2700.

For detailed information surrounding all facilities and activities within Olympic Park call or visit the **Homebush Bay Olympic Park Visitor Centre**, 1 Herb Elliot Ave, near the Olympic Park Railway Station, **T** 9714 7888, www.oca.nsw.gov.au, *0900-1700 daily*. It has a video-presentation, maps, displays, tour details and Olympic Games information.

Parramatta Heritage and Visitor Information Centre is at 346a Church St, Parramatta. **T** 9630 3703, www.parracity.nsw.gov.au *Mon-Fri 1000-1700, Sat and Sun 1000-1600*. A free brochure, *Discover Parramatta*, is very useful.

In Penrith, **Penrith Visitor Information Centre** is in Panthers Car park, Mulgoa Rd, Penrith, **T** 4732 7671, wwwpenrithvalley.com.au *0900-1630 daily*.

The **Manly Visitor Information Centre T** 9977 1088, www.manly.nsw.gov.au *1000-1600 daily*, is on the forecourt next to the ferry terminal. It is well stocked with detailed leaflets covering everything from eating out to bicycle hire and the staff will enthusiastically give a quick run down of the major sights and attractions on offer beyond the natural lure of the beach.

Blue Mountains

If approaching from the west, stop at the Glenbrook VIC to begin with and stock up with the free visitors' guide and maps. All regional centres also offer a free accommodation bookings service.

Glenbrook Visitor Information Centre is located just off the Great Western Highway in Glenbrook, **T** 1300 653 408, www.bluemountainstourism.org.au *Mon-Fri 0900-1700, Sat and Sun 0830-1630*.

Katoomba Visitor Information Centre is at Echo Point, **T** 1300 653 408, www.bluemountainstourism.org.au *0900-1700 daily*. The **Backpackers Travel Centre** is at 283 Main St, **T** 4782 5342.

NPWS Blue Mountains Heritage Centre is near the terminus of Govetts Leap Rd, Blackheath, **T** 4787 8877, www.npws.nsw.gov.au *0900-1630 daily*. They stock books, maps, gifts and offer extensive information on national parks and walks.

Hawkesbury River region

The accredited Visitors Information Centres in **Clarendon**, (Ham Common, Bicentenary Park, **T** 4588 5895, or **Brooklyn**, 2/5 Bridge St, **T** 9985 7090, www.hawkesbury-river.com.au, have detailed information on this area and other attraction and activities in the Hawkesbury River area. Local information is available in the **Coffee House** on Old Northern Rd, **T** 9651 4411. *0900-1700 daily*.

Ku-ring-gai Chase National Park
NPWS Bobbin Head Information Centre, Bobbin Inn, Bobbin Head Rd (western side of the park), **T** 9472 8949, *1000-1600 daily*, can supply walks, camping information and maps. There is also a gift shop. Ranger guided walks are often available.

Kalkari Visitors Centre, Chase Rd (between Mt Colah and Bobbin Head), **T** 9457 9853, *0900-1700 daily*, is another good source of information and maps.

Royal National Park
NPWS Royal National Park Visitors Centre, Farnell Ave, **T** 9542 0648, *0830-1630 daily*.

Botany Bay National Park
NPWS Botany Bay National Park Discovery Centre, Cape Solander Dr, **T** 9668 9111. *Mon-Fri 1100-1500, Sat and Sun 1000-1630* In the southern sector of the park, it is a good source of park and walks information and hosts an interesting display surrounding Cook's landing as well as the usual natural history.

Circular Quay and The Rocks 41

Heart, historical soul and transport hub. Hordes pay homage to the Opera House, harbour and bridge.

City Centre: the CBD 52

High-rises with manic, corporate corridors hide historical gems and retail therapy.

Darling Harbour and Chinatown 62

Smart Darling Harbour has waterside restaurants and bars, while Chinatown is all chatter, cheap shops and chicken chow mein.

City West: Glebe to Parramatta 71

The emancipated suburbs of Glebe and Newtown are laid-back, bohemian and cosmopolitan while Parramatta takes pride in its history and rugby.

City East: Kings Cross to Bondi 79

The red-lights of the Cross merge with the extrovert gay flamboyance of Darlinghurst, while Oxford Street stretches east to beachside suburbs.

City North: Manly to the Northern Beaches 86

Discrete harbour bays and a successful mix of his-and-her garages, manicured gardens, a zoo and generous portions of sand, surf and fish and chips.

Circular Quay and The Rocks

*As well as serving as the city's principal hub of transportation, Circular Quay draws sightseers like bees to honey. And how sweet it is to soak up the sights and the atmosphere of the **Opera House** and the **Harbour Bridge,** and to join the manic activity of the inner harbour. There are numerous harbour cruises, activities like the BridgeClimb and the quay's trendy restaurants. A simple walk between the Opera House via **Opera Quays** to the historic and commercial Rocks area provides the perfect venue to linger, take photographs or pause to enjoy the many bizarre street performers that come and go with the tides. Other quay attractions below the mighty high rises include the art deco **Museum of Contemporary Art**, **Customs House** and the **Justice and Police Museum**. What is most remarkable about **The Rocks** – on the western fringe of Circular Quay – is its transformation through time, from being a place rife with crime, prostitution, rum-fuelled street fights and even an outbreak of bubonic plague in 1900, to the orderly, healthy and highly presentable tourist attraction it is today.*

➧ *See Sleeping p122, Eating and drinking p146, Bars and clubs p169*

 Sights

★ **Sydney Opera House**
Macquarie St, Circular Quay, **T** 9250 7777, www.soh.nsw.gov.au
Mon-Sat 0900-2030. For latest performance schedules contact the SOH Box Office in the main foyer. $30-180 depending on prestige and your seat. Bookings essential (on-line bookings available). Entrance at other times free, tours extra (see below). Map 2, B8, p249

Even for the fiercest sceptics of man-made invention and architecture, who believe nothing made of human brain or brawn can match anything in nature – like the natural Australian icons of

In Sydney Harbour… the yachts will be racing on the crushed diamond water under a sky the texture of powdered sapphires. It would be churlish not to concede that the same abundance of natural blessings which gave us the energy to leave has every right to call us back.

Clive James
Born 1939
Australian critic, poet, novelist and broadcaster
From Unreliable Memoirs *(1980)*

Uluru (Ayers Rock) or the Great Barrier Reef for example – the magnificent Sydney Opera House cannot fail to impress. Almost 24 hours a day, every day, since this bizarre edifice was opened people have flocked to admire it, touch it, photograph it and even play on it, often without even a thought of its impressive interior or principal function. Built in 1973, it is the result of the Danish architect, Jorn Utzon's revolutionary design. In many ways it is like some futuristic cathedral with naves both inside and out, yet with an interior functioning not as a focus for ecclesiastical congregations and tradition, but for the best of national and international performing arts. The Opera House has five performance venues ranging from the main, 2,690 capacity Concert Hall to the small Playhouse Theatre. Combined, these host about 2,500 performances annually with everything from Bach to Billy Connolly. The Opera House is also the principal performance venue for Opera Australia, The Australian Ballet and Sydney Dance Company, the Sydney Symphony Orchestra and the Sydney Theatre Company.

There are also three **tours** and performance packages available. The *Front of House Tour* provides an insider's view of selected theatres and foyers; the *Backstage Pass*, as the name suggests, takes you behind the scenes and there is also the historical *Bennelong Walk*. The tours are available on a regular basis between 0830-1700 daily and take about 45 minutes with some having to fit around performances or rehearsals. Prices range from $15.40-25.20. The *Performance Package* combines a range of performance, dining and tour options. An SOH store selling official souvenirs, cafés, bars and a restaurant are also located within the complex.

● *The Opera House is best viewed not only intimately from close up, but also from afar. Some of the best spots are from Macquarie Point (end of the Domain on the western edge of farm Cove), especially at dawn, and from the* Park Hyatt Hotel *on the eastern edge of Circular Quay. Also, any ferry trip west bound from Circular Quay will reveal the structure in many of its multifaceted forms. From directly above the symmetrical design is impressive but without taking an expensive scenic flight this view will elude you.*

Justice and Police Museum

Corner Albert St and Phillip St, Circular Quay, **T** 9252 1144, www.hht.nsw.gov.au *Sat and Sun 1000-1700, daily in January. $7, children $3, family $17. Map 2, E6, p248*

Housed in the former 1856 Water Police Court, the Justice and Police Museum features, a magistrate's court and former police cells, as well as a gallery, and historical displays, showcasing the antics and fate of some of Sydney's most notorious criminals. The forensic evidence surrounding some of the most serious crimes, and the rather incriminating 'mug-shots' of the perpetrators, is interesting, but it is the impressive collection of weaponry that provides the most chilling reminder of their intent, attitude and determination.

Opera Quays

2 East Circular Quay, **T** 9247 9788, www.operaquays.com.au *Map 2, C7, p249*

At the eastern edge of the quay the new Opera Quays facade provides many tempting, but expensive, cafés and restaurants as well as an art gallery and a cinema.

Customs House

31 Alfred St, Circular Quay, **T** 9247 2285, *www.sydneycustomshouse.com.au Map 2, E6, p248*

Facing Circular Quay is the former 1840 Customs House which now houses several exhibition spaces, café/bars and on the fifth floor, the popular Café Sydney, a mainly seafood restaurant with superb views across the harbour. The Object Galleries (third floor) lends itself to craft and design, while on the fourth floor, the City Exhibition Space showcases historical and contemporary aspects of the city with a 1:500 model of the CBD being its main attraction.

Museum Of Contemporary Art

140 George St, The Rocks, **T** 9241 5892, www.mca.com.au *1000-1700 daily, free with a small charge for some temporary exhibitions, tours available Mon-Fri 1100 and 1400, Sat and Sun 1200 and 1330. Map 2, C5, p248*

At the southwestern corner of Circular Quay it is hard to miss the rather grand art deco Museum Of Contemporary Art. Opened in 1991 it houses a collection of some of Australia's best contemporary works, together with works by renowned international artists like Warhol and Hockney. The museum also hosts regular national and international exhibitions. Overlooking the quay the in-house *MCA Café* is a popular spot for lunch or a caffeine fix.

● *Along the main walkway of Circular Quay between the Museum of Contemporary Art and the Opera House, look out for the '****Writers Walk****' which is a series of plaques on the main concourse that quote famous Australian writers and celebrities. Contemporary writer and celebrity Clive James describes the water on the harbour as being like 'crushed diamonds'.*

Cadman's Cottage

110 George St, The Rocks, **T** 9247 5033, www.npws.nsw.gov.au *Mon-Fri 0930-1630, Sat and Sun 1000-1630. Free. Map 2, C5, p248*

A little further towards the Harbour Bridge is Cadman's Cottage that now sits somewhat out of place overlooking the futuristic Cruiseliner Terminal. The cottage, built in 1816, is the oldest surviving residence in Sydney and was originally the base for Governor Macquarie's boat crew, before playing host to the

Sydney Water Police. The cottage is named after the coxswain of the boat crew, John Cadman, a former convict sent to Australia, apparently, for stealing a horse. Worse still, his evil and despicable wife Elizabeth was found guilty of stealing a hairbrush.

The cottage is now home for the far less heinous staff of the **Sydney Harbour National Park Information Centre**, which is the main booking office and departure point for a number of harbour and island tours. A small historical exhibition is housed on the lower level. Admission is free.

The Rocks

For tours of the area, see p35. For further information on the rocks visit the Sydney VIC, 106 George Street (see p35), or www.rocksvillage.com
Map 2, C/B5, p248

Straddling the Bradfield Highway that now carries a constant flow of traffic across the Harbour Bridge, the historic Rocks village was the first site settled by European convicts and troops as early as 1788. Despite being given a major facelift in recent decades and managing to leave its reputation as the haunt of prostitutes, drunks and criminals to the history books, it still retains much of its original architectural charm and now serves as one of Sydney's most popular modern day tourist attractions. Both old and new is married, quite successfully, in an eclectic array of shops, galleries arcades, cafés and some mighty fine pubs and restaurants. It is a great place to spend a morning or afternoon wandering about, sightseeing, shopping or to dine – provided you can stand the constant sight of toy koalas and didgeridoos.

! It is not entirely unusual to see a penguin dodging the wakes of boats in the inner harbour. Blue penguins live and breed in Sydney Harbour and at the harbour mouth. In late winter and spring, migrating humpback whales are also regularly seen.

★ **Harbour Lights**
*Sydney Harbour, famous for its firework displays, puts on a
spectacular show every night as boats pass in and out of Circular
Quay, between the Opera House and The Rocks.*

The **Rocks Market** held every weekend (*1000-1700*) is perhaps
the most popular in Sydney and features a fine array of authentic
arts, crafts, bric-a-brac and souvenirs. But bear in mind it is always
very busy and subsequently both cramped and exhausting.

For live entertainment head for The **Rocks Square** in the heart
of the village where every day from 1200-1400 you'll find jazz,
classical or contemporary/traditional music on offer. Also look out
for two very camp and entertaining gentlemen on scooters,
dressed as policeman with skin-tight jodhpurs, leather boots and
with blue flashing lights on their heads: they may well caution you
for being in possession of boring attire or a bad haircut.

Children especially will love **The Rocks Toy Museum** housed
in the former 1854 Coachhouse on 2-6 Kendall Lane, see p217. It
boasts over 3,000 toys spanning two centuries. Also in Kendall

▶ BridgeClimb

The most high-profile activity in the city is the award-winning *BridgeClimb*, which involves the ascent of the 134-m Harbour Bridge span. For the vast majority of its 70-year life the huge 52, 800 tonne network of metal girders were the domain of engineers, maintenance crews and painters, but in recent years some bright spark has come up with the idea of guiding public groups to its heady, windswept crown. The three-hour climb can be done day or night and in most weather conditions, besides electrical storms. Before setting out you are suitably garbed and given a thorough safety briefing. Many say that as well as the stunning views from the top it is the excitement of getting there that is most memorable. Although it is fairly easy going and is regularly done by the elderly the sight and noise of the traffic below adds a special edge. Note that for safety reasons you cannot take your own camera on the trip and photographs of your group will be taken at the top. *BridgeClimb* headquarters is at 5 Cumberland Street, The Rocks, 0700-1900. Climbs during the week cost from from $130, children $100, weekends $160, children $125. Night climbs during the week cost from $160, children $125, at weekends $180, children $150. **T** 8274 7777.

Lane is the even more child-friendly **Puppet Theatre** that offers free shows at 1100,1230 and 1400 weekends and daily during school holidays, see p217.

To escape the crowds, head up Argyle Street, and the steps to Cumberland Street, taking a quick peek at the historic row of cottages at **Susannah Place**, 58-64 Gloucester Street, west side, below the popular Australian Hotel and pub, *Sat and Sun 1000-1700, Adult $7, children $3, family $17*, before walking through the pedestrian walkway to **Observatory Park**.

The park offers some fine views of the bridge and is home to the **Sydney Observatory**, Australia's oldest. There is an interesting exhibition covering early Aboriginal and European astronomy as well as evening tours offering a chance to view the heavens.

Almost next-door is the **SH Ervin Gallery**, at the National Trust Centre that has a reputation for hosting some fine, small-scale exhibitions. *Tue-Fri 1100-1700, Sat and Sun 1200-1700, Adults $6, child $4.*

From Observatory Park it is a short walk further along Argyle Street to enjoy a libation and a bite to eat at the *Lord Nelson*, one of Sydney's oldest pubs, (corner Kent and Argyle streets) before perhaps walking north down Lower Fort Street to **Dawes Point Park** with its dramatic bridge perspectives. At 43 Lower Fort Street, you may like to dip in to **Clydebank**, a restored mansion with period furnishings and a collection of former Rocks memorabilia. *Wed-Sat 1000-1800, $8.*

★ **Harbour Bridge**
Map 2, A5, p248

From near or far, above or below, day or night, it is impressive and imposing, however and from wherever you look at it. Sydney Harbour Bridge, or the 'Coat-hanger' as it is often called, was opened in 1932, taking nine years to build. The deck supports eight lanes of traffic (accommodating around 150,000 vehicles a day), a railway line and a pedestrian walkway, which, along with the more recent 'out of sight, out of mind' subterranean Harbour Tunnel below, forms a crucial artery to the North Shore and beyond.

For over six decades the best views from the bridge were accessed by foot from its 59-m high deck, but now the **BridgeClimb** experience, that ascends the 134-m high, 502-m long span, has developed in to an award-winning Sydney experience, see box, p48.

Not as thrilling, but far cheaper, are the views on offer from the top of the **Southeastern Pylon Lookout**, which can be accessed from the eastern walkway and Cumberland Street, The Rocks. The pylon also houses the **Harbour Bridge Exhibition**.

From below the best views of the bridge are from **Hickson Rd** and **Deans Point** (south side) and **Milsons Point** (north side).

Harbour islands

For all island access, tour information and bookings contact the Sydney Harbour National Park Information Centre, Cadman's Cottage, 110 George St, The Rocks, T 9247 5033, www.npws.nsw.gov.au Mon-Fri 0900-1630, Sat and Sun 1000-1630. Map 1, p251

Sydney harbour is scattered with a number of interesting islands most of which hold some historical significance. **Fort Denison**, just east of the Opera House, is the smallest, the most obvious and by far the most notorious. Its proper name is Pinchgut Island and it is so called because it was originally used as an open-air jail and a place where inmates were abandoned for a week and supplied with nothing except bread and water, often for little more than stealing another inmates biscuits. Furthermore, in 1796, the then Governor of NSW left a sobering warning to the new penal colony by displaying the body of executed murderer Francis Morgan from a gibbet on the island's highest point. The island was later converted to a fort in the 1850s in fear of a Russian invasion during the Crimean war. There is a café on site and two tours are available. The *Brunch Tour*, Saturday 0900-1200, Sunday 0915-1200, $47, children $43 and the *Heritage Tour*, Monday to Friday 1130-1515 and 1500-1715, Saturday 1130-1515 and 1500-1650, Sunday 1130-1500 and 1440-1650, $22, children $18.

Spans and spanners

The Sydney Harbour Bridge concedes the title of the world's longest single span bridge to New York's Bayonne Bridge, which beats it by a spanner's length.

A little further east, off Darling Harbour, is **Clark Island**, a popular picnic retreat. East again, off Rose Bay, is **Shark Island**, so called because of its shape. It served as a former animal quarantine centre and public reserve, before becoming part of the Sydney Harbour National Park in 1975.

West of the bridge is the largest of the harbour's islands, **Goat Island**, which is the site of a former, convict-built gunpowder station and barracks. This provides the venue for a range of entertaining tours including the *Gruesome Tales Tour*, Saturdays 1800-2130, $24.20 Adults only. It recounts the island's grisly past. There is also a standard *Heritage Tour*. Monday, Friday, Saturday and Sunday, 1300-1515, $19.80, children $15.40, family $61.60.

City Centre: the CBD

*A fine place to begin your exploration of Sydney's bustling CBD is on foot via the **Museum of Sydney** built over two centuries ago. Of equal appeal, however, are the diverse historical buildings along **Macquarie Street** including **Government House**, the **State Library of New South Wales**, the former **Sydney Hospital, Mint**, and the functioning **NSW Parliament House**. Right in the heart of the CBD the **State Theatre** and **Town Hall** reveal architecturally splendid interiors, while nearby, the **Queen Victoria Building** is a place where history meets retail therapy with almost equal appeal. For a bird's-eye view the **Sydney Tower**, another of the city's familiar icons, rarely disappoints, providing the weather is fine (which it usually is), while, for a rapid escape from the chaos, **Hyde Park** or the **Royal Botanical Gardens** can offer far more than welcome serenity and a convenient place to tuck in to that corporate-sized sandwich. For some detailed insight in to the vast lands beyond the city the cool and grandiose interior of the **Australian Museum** on the fringe of Hyde Park is well worth a visit, while the ecclesiastical architecture of **St Mary's Cathedral** nearby is also worth a look. Nestled neatly between the Hyde Park and the botanical gardens, **The Domain** offers its own high profile attraction and colour in the form of the **Art Gallery of New South Wales**.*

▸▸ *See Sleeping p123, Eating and drinking p148, Bars and clubs p170*

 Sights

Museum of Sydney

37 Philip St, **T** 9251 5988, www.hht.nsw.gov.au *0930-1700, $7, children $3, family $17. Map 2, E6, p248*

The Museum of Sydney (MOS) was opened in 1995 and is a clever and imaginative mix of old and new. It is built on the original site of 'First Fleet' captain Governor Phillip's 1788 residence and incorporates some of the original archaeological remains. It contains uncluttered and well-presented displays exploring the history and stories that surround the creation and development of the city, from the first indigenous settlers, through the European invasion and up to the modern day. Art is an important aspect of this museum and as well as dynamic and temporary exhibitions incorporating a city theme there are some permanent pieces, the most prominent being the *Edge of the Trees*, a sculptural installation that sits at the museum entrance. It is an intriguing concept and a clever mix of media and cultures, reflecting on the nature and substance of the city itself. There is a shop and café on site.

Government House

Macquarie St, **T** 9931 5222. *Fri-Sun 1000-1500 (grounds daily 1000-1600). Guided tours only within the house, departing every half hour from 1030. Free. Map 2, C8, p249*

Macquarie Street, forming the eastern fringe of the CBD, is Sydney's most historic street and the site of many original, important and impressive architectural establishment buildings. From north to south the first, set near the Opera House, in its own expansive grounds, is Government House, a Gothic revival building completed in 1837. The interior contains many period furnishings and features giving an insight in to the lifestyle of the former NSW Governors and their families.

State Library of New South Wales

Macquarie St, **T** 9273 1414, www.slnsw.gov.au *Mon-Fri 0900-2100, Sat and Sun 1100-1700, (Mitchell Library closed Sundays), $16 for visiting exhibitions. Map 2, G7, p249*

Facing the Botanical gardens on Macquarie Street is the State Library of New South Wales. Its architecture speaks for itself, but housed within its walls are some very significant historical documents, including eight out of the ten known First Fleeter diaries. Also worth a look is one of the three intricate Melocco Brothers mosaic floor decorations that exist in the city. In this instance the foyer floor of the Mitchell Library entrance depicts the journey of Dutch explorer Abel Tasman in 1642-43. The library also hosts temporary exhibitions that are almost always worth visiting and offers an on-going programme of films, workshops and seminars. There is a shop and café on site.

Sydney Hospital, Parliament House and The Royal Mint

Free tours are offered when Parliament is not in session, and when it is you can visit the public gallery. Map 2, H/G7, p249

Next door to the State Library, the original north wing of the 1816 Sydney Hospital (formerly known as the Rum Hospital) is now the NSW Parliament House. Quite often the house becomes the focus for lively demonstrations that often terminate here after a procession through the city streets. The south wing of the hospital gave way to the Royal Mint in 1854 during the gold rush. No wonder it was called the Rum Hospital: with a plague of politicians on one side, locked up gold on the other and a large crowd outside, screaming like banshees, it would turn any sick teetotaller into a raging alcoholic.

Hyde Park Barracks

Queens Sq, Macquarie St, **T** 92238922, www.hht.nsw.gov.au
0930-1700 daily. $7, children $3, Family $17. Sydney Explorer Bus route, stop 4. Map 2, H7, p249

The barracks, which lie on the northern fringe of Hyde Park, were commissioned in 1816 by Governor Macquarie to house male convicts before being utilized later as an orphanage and an asylum. The renovated buildings now house a modern museum

Tall towers

Sydney is now the economic centre of a region which stretches all the way to Southeast Asia. The office buildings of the city centre crowd around a scattering of older buildings .

that displays the history of the Barracks, the grisly aspects of exiled convict life, and the work of the architect Francis Greenway. Guided tours are available, with the unusual added option of staying overnight in convict hammocks. Café on site.

Sydney (Centrepoint) Tower

100 Market St, **T** 9231 9300 (restaurant bookings **T** 8223 3800), www.centreponit.com.au   *Observation Deck Sun-Fri 0900-2230, Sat 0900-2330, $19.80, children $13.20, family $55, virtual tour extra. Map 3, A5, p250*

Rising from a manic buzz of retail therapy, the Sydney (Centrepoint) Tower, has, since 1981, been an instantly recognisable landmark across the city. After the Opera House and Harbour Bridge the Sydney Tower is considered the city's third great icon, forming a diverse trio. The tower's 2,239-tonne golden turret is also known as *Ned's Helmet* due to its resemblance to the famous Aussie bushranger (highwayman) Ned Kelly's protective headgear.

Although aged in comparison to the futuristic Sky Tower, in Auckland, New Zealand (which on completion in 1995 pipped the Sydney Tower at 305 m by just a few metres) the view from Australia's highest building is no less impressive. As well as enjoying the stunning vistas from the tower's **Observation Deck**, you can also experience a virtual 'Great Australian Expedition' tour, or dine in one of two revolving restaurants (sadly, they only revolve sedately every 70 minutes). Given the elevated price of entry to the Observation Deck, you should keep an eye on the weather forecast and pick a clear day.

State Theatre
49 Market St, **T** 9373 6861. *$12, concessions $8. Self-guided tours available Mon-Fri, 1130-1500* Map 3, A4, p250

Between the Sydney Tower and the Queen Victoria Building it is worth taking a peek at the impressive interior of the 1929 State Theatre. Much of its charm is instantly on view in the entrance foyer, but it is perhaps the 20,000 piece glass chandelier and Wurlitzer organ housed in the auditorium that steals the show.

Queen Victoria Building (QVB)
455 George St, **T** 9267 4761, www.qvb.com.au *Mon-Wed, Fri and Sat 0900-1800, Thu 0900-2100, Sun 1100-1700 (some restaurants and cafés remain open after hours). Information desks on the ground floor and level 2 dome area. Guided tours available twice daily,* **T** *9264 9209. Explorer bus stop 14.* Map 3, B4, p250

Just around the corner from the State Theatre on George Street boldly taking up an entire city block is the grand Queen Victoria Building. Built in 1898 to celebrate Queen Victoria's Golden Jubilee

QVB

Another example of an Australian penchant for abbreviation, the Queen Victoria Building is as famous for its clocks as its shops.

and to replace the original Sydney Markets, the QVB (as it is known) is most often touted as a prime **shopping** venue, containing three floors of boutique outlets, and selling everything from designer knickers to Aboriginal art. But shopping aside, the spectacular interior is well worth a look, with ornate architecture, stained-glass windows, mosaics and two charming and intricate automata turret clocks. At the northern end, the four-tonne **Great Australian Clock** is the world's largest hanging animated turret clock. A stunning creation, it took four years to build at a cost of $1.5 million. Once activated with a $4 donation the clock comes alive with moving picture scenes and figurines that would put any flock of operatic canaries to shame. At the southern end is the equally impressive **Royal Clock,** with its English historical theme. Among the many animated depictions is the execution of King Charles I, whose head goes up and down like a yoyo 12 times a day. There are also a number of good galleries.

Town Hall and St Andrew's Cathedral

Corner of George and Druitt sts. **T** 9265 9007. *0900-1700 daily. Free. Explorer bus stop 14. Self-guided tour brochure available in the foyer. Map 3, C4/B4, p250*

Across the street from the QVB is the Town Hall, built in 1888. It also has an impressive interior, the highlight of which is the 8,000-pipe organ, reputed to be the largest in the world. Next door to the Town Hall is the renovated St Andrew's Cathedral, built between 1819 and 1868. There are regular choir performances for which entry is free.

Hyde Park and surrounds

Explorer Bus route, stop 7. Map 3, D6-A6, p250

Hyde Park itself is very impressive and a fine mix of aesthetics from the historic grandeur of the 1932 **Archibald Fountain** and 1934 **Anzac War Memorial**, to the gracious sanctity of its spacious lawns and mighty corridor of trees. It provides a great place to escape the mania of the city and to people-watch. Here perhaps more than anywhere else in the city you will see a diverse mix of humanity, from camera-touting tourists to amorous lovers, from suits on a lunch-break to the homeless on a no-break.

St Mary's Cathedral

College St, **T** 9220 0400. *Free. Crypt 1000-1600 daily. Free tours Sun afternoons after mass at 1200. Explorer Bus route, stop 7. Map 3, A7, p251*

At the northeastern edge of Hyde Park on College Road is St Mary's Cathedral, which is well worth a look inside. It has an impressive and wonderfully peaceful interior, with the highlight being the Melocco Brothers mosaic floor in the crypt that depicts The Creation and took 16 years to complete.

Australian Museum

6 College St, **T** 9320 6000, www.austmus.gov.au *0930-1700, $8, children $3, family $19, (special exhibitions extra). Explorer Bus route, stop 7. Map 3, C7, p251*

A little further south along College Street is the Australian Museum established in 1827. Considering the huge demands placed upon museums these days to keep the computer-age public satisfied by being at the cutting edge of technology, presentation and entertainment, the Australian Museum gets a credit, if not the gold star. The *Modern Biodiversity* and *Indigenous Australians* displays are well up with the play, but sadly the *Birds and Insects* section lets the side down. There, the numerous stuffed specimens still support those traditional taxidermy facial expressions of the persecuted being electrocuted, with several of the largest looking like they have a direct link to the mains. Also housed in the museum is the magnificent *Chapman Mineral Collection* that has just about every 'ite' and 'zite' that syllables could possibly bond with. The colours and diversity are mind blowing and you'll never view a rock in the same way again. Coincide your visit to the *Indigenous Australian* section with the live didgeridoo playing and informative lectures given by Aboriginal staff.

● *Children and anyone with a healthy sense of inquisition will also love the impressive Search and Discover section.*

Royal Botanical Gardens

Mrs Macquarie's Rd via Art Gallery Rd, **T** 9231 8111, www.rbgsyd.gov.au *0700-sunset. Free. Tropical Centre daily 1000-1600, $5. Explorer Bus route, stop 3. Map 2, F7-C11, p249*

The 30-hectare Royal Botanical Gardens offers a wonderful sanctuary of peace and greenery only a short stroll east of the city centre and has done so for almost 200 years. It boasts a fine array of mainly native plants and trees, an intriguing pyramid-shaped Tropical House, rose and succulent gardens, rare and threatened species and decorative ponds. However, it is, without doubt, its large colony of wild flying foxes (bats) that is most absorbing. During the day they roost in their hundreds in the heart of the gardens, hanging on almost available crowning tree branch, like black and gold Christmas decorations, moving only now and again to groom, stretch a wing or argue with their neighbour. So close to a bustling city centre, replete with so many human urban icons, it really is an incredible sight that will have you either running a mile or staring heavenward in awe. There is a **Visitors Centre** and shop located near Art Gallery Road in the southeastern corner of the park. There you can pick up a self-guided walks tour leaflet or join a free organized **tour** at 1300 daily. A specialist *Aboriginal Tour*, that explores the significance of the site to the Cadigal (the original Aboriginal inhabitants) and the first European settler's desperate attempts to cultivate the site is available on request, $16.50, **T** 9231 8050.

● *The Gardens Café and Restaurant, right in the heart of the gardens, is one of the best places to observe the bats – just follow the faint, musty smell. Bats are fastidiously clean animals but are not designed to smell like us, or alas, roses.*

★ Macquarie Point
Mrs Macquarie's Rd. *Sydney Explorer Bus route, stop 5.*
Map 2, C11, p249

From the Botanical Gardens it is a short stroll to **Macquarie Point** and **Mrs Macquarie's Chair** and one of the best vistas of the Opera House and Harbour Bridge in the city. It is an especially good place to be at dawn or for sunset. As the name suggests, Mrs Macquarie's chair is the spot where the first Governor's wife came to reflect upon the new settlement, or perhaps yearn for her native Scotland. One can only imagine what her reaction would be now.

★ Art Gallery of New South Wales

Art Gallery Rd, The Domain, **T** 9225 1744, www.artgallery.nsw.gov.au
*1000-1700. Free (small charge for some visiting exhibitions). Explorer
Bus route stop 6.* Map 2, H8, p249

At the southeastern edge of the Botanical Gardens, and fronting
The Domain, is the Art Gallery of New South Wales, Australia's
largest. Housed behind its grand facade are the permanent works
of many of the country's most revered contemporary artists, as
well as a collection of more familiar international names like Monet
and Picasso. In stark contrast the Yiribana Gallery is a major
highlight, showcasing a fine collection of Aboriginal and Torres
Strait Islander works that are well worth a look. There are half-hour
dance and music performances in the gallery Tuesday to Saturday
at 1200. The main gallery also features a dynamic programme of
major visiting exhibitions. An extensive and no doubt aesthetically
dramatic expansion was being planned at the time of writing.

Be sure not to miss the quirky and monumental matchsticks
installation by **Brett Whitely** located outside, behind the main
building. Brett is one of the city's most celebrated artists whom,
until his recent death, produced a broad range of work, in mixed
media, that are like this piece, typically eccentric, unpretentious
and often humorous. More of Whitley's work can be seen at the
★ Brett Whitely Museum, 2 Raper Street, Surry Hills, see p82

The Domain

Art Gallery Rd. *Explorer Bus route stop 6.* Map 2, G/H 7/8, p249

The pleasant green expanse of tree and open park sitting between
the Art Gallery and Macquarie Place was declared a public domain
in 1810. It is often used as a free concert venue especially over
Christmas and during the Sydney Festival held every January.

Darling Harbour and Chinatown

*Revitalised for the city's bicentennial in 1988 and continuously developed ever since, Darling Harbour has become one of the most celebrated, diverse and most popular tourist venues in Sydney. The modern facades of its two main waterside attractions, the **Sydney Aquarium** and the **Australian Maritime Museum**, together with the **Sydney Fish Market** on its fringe, all provide fascinating insight, entertainment and a stark contrast to our own relationship with the ocean and the other creatures that make it their home. Elsewhere, a general emphasis on brash modern architecture, nightlife and entertainment is accentuated at the **Star City Casino**, where the melodic trickles of numerous water features fall like the tears of the luckless and the ruined. Other notable attractions include the **Powerhouse Museum**, with its remarkable plenitude of artefacts, the **IMAX Theatre**, with its own big bombardment of the senses, and a wealth of trendy restaurants, bars and nightclubs. In contrast, the **Chinese Garden of Friendship**, towards the southwestern fringe provides a little serenity before giving way to the old and chaotic enclave of **Chinatown**, the epicentre of Sydney's Asian community and a place where the hungry tourist meets the condemned lobster.*

▸▸ *See Sleeping p125, Eating and drinking p151, Bars and clubs p172*

 ## Sights

Sydney Aquarium

Aquarium Pier, Darling Harbour, **T** 9262 2300, www.sydneyaquarium.com.au   *0900-2000. $23, children $11, family $49 (Aquarium Pass with ferry from Circular Quay, $27.40, child $14.30). Explorer bus stop 21.   Map 2, H2, p248*

A modern, well-presented aquarium like Sydney, with over 650 species, cannot fail to impress. The thing about this aquarium is also the fact that it is not all fish. On show are imaginative habitat arenas, where saltwater crocodiles, frogs, seals, penguins and of course the bizarre and enchanting platypuses all await you. Without doubt the highlight of the aquarium is the Great Barrier Reef Oceanarium; a huge, superbly crafted and stocked tank with vast walls of glass that give you an incredible insight in to the world's largest living thing and the mind-bending array of other life that depends upon it. Of course, many visit the aquarium to come face to face with some of Australia's deadliest sea creatures, without getting their feet wet. There is no doubt that such beauty and diversity has its dark side, as the notorious box-jellyfish, cone shell, or rockfish will reveal.

National Maritime Museum

*2 Murray St, **T** 9298 3777, www.anmm.gov.au 0930-1700 daily. Tickets range according to the number of attractions, from the basic Gallery Pass at $10 to the Super Pass at $20, children $6- $10, family $25-$45. The Maritime Museum is easily reached by foot across the Pyrmont Bridge, or by Monorail, LightRail or the Sydney Explorer bus, stop 19. Map 2, H1, p248*

The National Maritime Museum, deliberately designed to look from the outside like the sails of a ship, offers a fine mix of old and new, in both diversity and scale. For many, its biggest attractions are the warship **MHS Vampire** and submarine **HMAS Onslow**, the centrepieces of a fleet of old vessels that sit outside on the harbour. Both can be thoroughly explored. Volunteer guides take you through the cramped interior. The interior of the museum contains a range of displays exploring Australia's close links with all things nautical, from the early navigators and the **First Fleet** and the ocean liners that brought many waves of immigrants, to commerce, the navy, sport and leisure. Other attractions include a café, shop, sailing lessons and a range of short cruises on a variety of historical vessels. Don't miss the beautifully-restored 1874

▶ Harbour cruises

There are a wealth of good value harbour cruises on offer with most being based at Circular Quay. Trips vary from a sedate cruise on a replica of the Bounty (see p151) to paddle steamers and fast catamarans. There are three principal companies offering a wide range of cruises on mainly modern craft: **Captain Cook** and **Sydney ferries**, based at Circular Quay and **Matilda**, based at Aquarium Wharf, Darling Harbour. Other companies offer cruises on older or specialist vessels, including the charismatic replica of *The Bounty, The Sydney Showboat Paddle Steamer, Ocean Spirit, The Majestic, The Americas Cup Spirit* and the 1874 *James Craig*. There are also some excellent cruises options up the Hawkesbury River from Palm Beach, north of Sydney, **T** 9997 4815.

Sydney Ferries offer a one-hour *Morning Cruise* from $15, children $7.50, family $37.50 (1000 and 1115 daily); a two hour 30 minute *Afternoon Cruise*, from $22, children $11, family $54 (daily 1300 and 1330) and a one hour 30 minute *Evening Harbour Lights Cruise*, $19, children $9.50, family $47.50 (Monday to Saturday 2000). All Cruises leave from Wharf 4. The morning and evening cruises ply the inner harbour sights while the afternoon tour also visits the Middle Harbour. A commentary is provided throughout and drinks are also available. The Harbour Jet and Jet Cats also cruise to Manly or up to Parramatta. **T** 131500, www.sydneytransport.net.au

Captain Cook have 12 large, modern catamarans and offer a wide range of cruises throughout the day and evening, often including lunch or dinner and entertainment. All cruises depart from Wharf 6. **T** 9206 1112, cruise@ captaincook.com.au Cruises range from $20, children $15, for a basic onehour 15 minute *Harbour Highlights Cruise* to

$99/$55 for a two hour 30 minute à la carte *Dinner Cruise*. All cruises depart from Wharf 6.

Matilda, based in Darling Harbour, offer morning, afternoon, lunch and dinner cruises aboard luxury catamarans. Cruises range in price from $27, children $13.70, for a one hour 40 minute morning cruise to $94, children $49.50, for a three hour dinner cruise. **T** 9264 7377, www.matilda.com.au

Majestic own and operate the Sydney Showboat Paddlesteamer fleet which are replicas of the original vessels that used to ply the harbour in the 1800s. A range of cruises are on offer from the basic one hour 30 minute *Harboursights*, from $19, children $11.40 (departs 1510, 1530, 1715) to the two-hour à la carte *Twilight Dinner Cruise*, from $85, children $51 (departs 1930). The steamers leave from Kings Street Wharf, Darling Harbour and pick up at the Eastern Pontoon in Circular Quay. **T** 9552 2722, www.bluelinecruises.com.au

The Spirit is a fairly new edition to the harbour fleet. She is an International America's Cup Class yacht from the 1992 San Diego Challenge. The three-hour cruise offers an exhilarating introduction to the world of yacht racing, from $94, **T** 9660 9133. No sailing experience is necessary.

If you are looking for a cruise with a difference maybe one in a comfortable amphibious vehicle will suffice. As they boast, it is after all the only harbour cruise that can go over the bridge as well as under it. Departs Clocktower Square, The Rocks Thursday to Monday at 1030, 1230 and 1430, from $50 For details contact **Aussie Duck**, **T** 131007, www.aussieduck.com

The VIC has listings of boat charters based in Sydney, many of which also offer whale watching trips from June to October.

square rigger, the **James Craig**, which is moored to the north of the museum at Wharf 7. After completion she will set sail again offering another historic cruise option.

Sky City Casino
Pirrama Rd, **T** 9777 9000, www.starcity.com.au *24 hrs. Best accessed by foot or by Monorail, LightRail or the Sydney Explorer bus, stop 19.*

Set back off the harbour and facing the city is the Sky City Casino. Even if you are not a gambler the complex is worth a visit, especially at night, when the many and varied water features that are incorporated into its curvaceous design spring to life in a water and light extravaganza. The casino is open 24 hours a day and there are also two theatres, a nightclub, restaurants, cafés and bars, a hotel and a health club.

★ Sydney Fish Market
Bank St, Pyrmont, **T** 9660 1611/ **T** 9552 2180, www.sydneyfishmarket.com.au *From 0600. Tours Mon-Fri from 0700. Sydney Light Rail or bus routes 443 from Circular Quay and 501 from Town Hall (or walk from Darling Harbour). Map 4, B5, p252*

For anyone interested in sea creatures, the spectacle of the Sydney Fish Market is highly recommended. It is a place where wildlife (albeit dead) and commercial trading combine in one fascinating arena. Every morning from 0530, over 2,700 crates of 100 species of seafood from fisherman's co-ops and aquaculture farms in NSW are sold to a lively bunch of 200 buyers using a computerised auction clock system. The best way to see the action, and more importantly the incredible diversity of species, is to join a tour group which will give you access to the auction floor. Normally the general public are confined to the viewing deck high above the floor, which, although giving an overview of the action, does not

Southeast Asia town
Sydney's Chinatown is actually the focus point for many of the city's Southeast Asian communities.

offer the same detail. Also within the market complex are cafés, some excellent seafood eateries and a superb range of open markets where seafood can be bought at competitive prices. The best time to get to the markets is about 0600. Things start to wind up at about 1000 when most tourists are as bleary eyed as the fish.

Powerhouse Museum

500 Harris St, Ultimo, **T** 9217 0111, www.phm.gov.au *1000-1700 daily. $10, children $3, family $23. Monorail, LightRail or Sydney Explorer bus stop 17.   Map 3, E1, p250*

When it comes to collections the Powerhouse Museum is exactly that: a powerhouse of nearly 400,000 items collected over 120 years. Of course only a fraction of these can be displayed at any one time, but there is undoubtedly something for everyone and it remains Australasia's largest museum and (according to itself) Sydney's most popular. Housed in the former Ultimo Power Station, there is an impressive range of memorabilia, from aircraft to musical instruments, mainly with an emphasis on Australian innovation and achievement, and covering a wide range of general topics from science and technology, to transportation, social history, fashion and design. Given its size and content you may need more than one trip, with half a day being barely enough to cover all the highly interactive displays. There is a shop and café on site.

Motor World

320 Harris St, **T** 9552 3375 Pyrmont. *Wed-Sun 1000-1700, $10, children $5, family $20.*

Only a short walk from the Powerhouse Museum is Motor World, where car buffs can drool over more than 150 rare and everyday vehicles, motorcycles and automotive memorabilia.

IMAX Theatre

Darling Harbour, **T** 9281 3300, www.imax.com.au *1000-2200, $16.20, children $10.80, family $38, Explorer bus stop 22. Map 3, B2, p250*

Next door to the Darling Harbour VIC, on the Cockle Bay waterfront is the eight-storey IMAX Theatre, which shows several one-hour films, with some in 3D, from 1000 daily.

Australia's Northern Territory and Outback Centre

Darling Harbour, **T** 9283 7477, www.outbackcentre.com.au *1000-1900 daily. Performances Tue-Fri 1300, 1500 and 1700, Sat and Sun 1300,1400, 1500 and 1700. Map 3, D1, p250*

Facing Tumbalong Park in the southern section of Darling Harbour, and next door to the Chinese Garden, this is little more than a glorified souvenir shop with a free 30-minute live show presenting outback imagery and featuring didgeridoo playing in order to lure in the crowds. If you intend going to the Northern Territory there is also a specialist travel shop and booking agent.

Waterscreens

Wed-Sun every half hour from 1930. Map 3, B1, p250

Darling Harbour is spectacular at night when the Waterscreens show springs to life with a light and music spectacular, using multicoloured lasers projected on to two, fine mist fountains in the middle of Cockle Bay. Shows alternate using classical, jazz and popular music and the animated images are excellent.

Chinatown
Map 3, E3, p250

Further along George Street and occupying the southwestern corner of the CBD is the Haymarket district and Chinatown. The Chinese have been an integral part of Sydney culture since the Gold Rush of the mid 1800s, though today Chinatown is also the focus of many other Asian cultures, including Vietnamese, Thai, Korean and Japanese. The district offers a lively diversion, with its heart being the Dixon Street pedestrian precinct, between the two pagoda gates facing Goulburn Street and Hay Street.

● *Here, and in the surrounding streets, you will find a wealth of Asian shops and restaurants, many of which stay open well past midnight.*

Chinese Garden of Friendship
Corner of Harbour and Pier Sts, **T** 9281 6863. *0930-dusk daily. $4.50, children $2, families $10. Map 3, D1/2, p250*

At the northwestern corner of Chinatown is the Chinese Garden of Friendship, which was gifted to NSW by her sister Chinese province, Guangdong, to celebrate the Australian Bicentenary in 1988. It contains beautiful craftsmanship and landscaping, including a teahouse that provides the ideal sanctuary from the stresses of the city.

Paddy's Market
T 1300 361 589, www.paddysmarkets.com.au *Fri, Sat, Sun 0900-1630. On the corner of Hay and Thomas Streets. Map 3, F2/3, p250*

Paddy's Market is one of Sydney's largest, oldest and liveliest markets. It is also one of the tackiest.

City West: Glebe to Parramatta

*As well as some superb people-watching opportunities the free-spirited western suburbs of **Glebe** and **Newtown** both offer the chance to happen upon everything from secondhand books to pink boob tubes, or even treat yourself to a massage or a mud spa, all before your stomach demands a more serious perusal of the enormous range of Newtown's international menus. Good food is also the principal attraction in **Leichhardt**, Sydney's Little Italy, with the best (and best value) pasta or gelato in the city. Not to be outdone, **Balmain**, fringing the harbour and occupying a headland just to the north of Glebe, is fast metamorphosing from a rather drab working class suburb, with a paucity of attractions, into the latest forerunner in Sydney's growing list of chic and happening suburban retreats. Further west (and best reached with a scenic trip along the harbour by Jetcat or ferry) **Olympic Park** remains a major attraction long after the flame of competition has been extinguished. While possessing far less appeal, **Parramatta** still hides some of the city's (and the state's) most important historical assets.*

▶▶ *See Sleeping p126, Eating and drinking p153, Bars and clubs p176*

 Sights

Balmain

Balmain can be reached by buses 441-444 from the QVB, or by ferry from Circular Quay, Wharf 5. Map 1, p251

Straddling Johnstons Bay and connecting Darling Harbour and Pyrmont with the peninsula suburb of Balmain is Sydney's second landmark bridge, the **Anzac Bridge**, opened in 1995. It is a modern, strangely attractive edifice, that although unable to win a battle of aesthetics over the mighty Harbour Bridge, still makes an admirable attempt. Just beyond its spoke-like suspensions, the former working-class suburb of Balmain is most often recognised in name, rather than location, as one of Australia's best-known rugby league teams. In recent years Balmain has undergone a quiet evolution from a nondescript moth to a vibrant butterfly. Now it seems Balmain loves nothing more than to flutter its new and colourful wings like a drag queen does her eyelashes. As a result Balmain, and in particular Darling Street, now boasts a small but eclectic range of gift shops, modern cafés, restaurants and pubs, which by road, or preferably by ferry from Circular Quay, provide a pleasant escape from the city centre.

● *Balmain has hosted a popular Saturday market in the grounds of St Andrew's Church, on the corner of Darling Street and Curtis Street, for over two decades.*

Glebe and Newtown

Glebe can be reached by buses 431 or 434 from George St in the city . Newtown can be reached by buses 422, 423 and 426-428 from Loftus St (Circular Quay) or George St in the city . The Newtown Railway Station is on the Inner West/Bankstown (to Liverpool) lines.
Map 4, p252

To the southwest of Darling Harbour, beyond Ultimo, and separated by the campus of **Sydney University** (Australia's oldest), are Glebe and Newtown. Glebe prides itself in having an alternative New Age village atmosphere, where a cosmopolitan, mainly student crowd amble along its main drag Glebe Point Road to meet in the laid-back cafés, peruse in old style bookshops or bohemian fashion outlets, or seek the latest therapies in alternative health shops.

The **Saturday market** provides an outlet for local crafts people to sell their work, as well as a mix of bric-a-brac, clothes and New Age essentials in the grounds of Glebe Public School, Glebe Point Road. *Mon 1100-1230, Sun 1100-1145.*

▶ Snaps

Circular Quay and the great icons of the Harbour Bridge and Opera House offer endless opportunities and perspectives. The best locations from which to capture the scale and angular complexities of the Harbour Bridge are from close up and below on Hickson's Rd and around Dawes Point Park (southern end) and from Milson's Point (northern end). Both of these areas are especially good at dawn and at dusk. Observatory Park is an excellent place from which to shoot the brightly-lit bridge at night. For other great views of the bridge, the harbour and the city centre, climb to the lookout on the southeastern tower (1000-1700).

The colourful activity of Circular Quay is best tackled from its main concourse or from the elevation of the Cahill Express Walkway.

The Opera House offers superb opportunities. From afar, try Campbells Cove, Circular Quay (Park Hyatt Hotel), late in the day and from Mrs Macquaries Point at dawn. Hyde Park is excellent for city views.

The city centre can also provide interesting human and high-rise building perspectives. While you are there, don't miss the interior of the QVB building on George Street.

From George Street wander through Haymarket and Chinatown, before tackling the vast architectural opportunities around Darling Harbour.

Cockle Bay and The Star City complex are excellent locations for colourful night shots. Around sunset the cityscape from Rozelle, with the Anzac Bridge in the foreground, also offers some interesting vistas. Bondi Beach, Bronte and Manly Beach are all excellent when at their busiest at weekends, or for a change, at dawn. Homebush Bay Olympic Park is great for modern architecture, while Macquarie Street in the city is best for more traditional buildings.

▶ Flights of fancy

Although the sights of Sydney blow you away with your feet firmly planted on the ground, seeing it from above can be even more exhilarating and provide an entirely different aspect, especially of icons like the Opera House. There are a number of fixed-wing and helicopter scenic flight companies including **Sydney Heli-Aust**, **T** 9317 3402, www.heliaust.com.au that offer 30-minute (from $150) to 35 minute (from $199) helicopter flights around the inner harbour and five-hour luncheon trips to the Hunter Valley (from $599). They are based at the airport but offer pick-ups from the city. An interesting alternative are the scenic flights offered by **Sydney Seaplanes** **T** 1300 656 787, www.sydneybyseaplane.com.au based in Rose Bay. They offer a 15-minute flight around the harbour from $120, children $60, while a 90-minute trip taking in the harbour, beaches and Blue Mountains costs from $620, children $310. Other companies include **Sydney Harbour Seaplanes**, **T** 1800 803 558, www.sydneyseaplanes.com.au also based in Rose Bay.

South beyond the university is **King Street**, the hub of Newtown's almost bizarre and cosmopolitan range of shops, cafés and restaurants. Here you can purchase anything from a black leather cod-piece to an industrial-sized brass budda, dribble over the menus of a vast range of interesting eateries, or simply sit over a latte, feeling hopelessly boring and conservative, while watching the world go by wearing anything from skintight pink boob tubes and flared trousers to kipper ties, colourful beanies and Earth-calling-mother-ship sunglasses. A half-day wander, a Sunday brunch, or an evening meal in Newtown's King Street, is highly recommended. It shakes the nipple tassels off Kings Cross and is far less commercial or outwardly sleazy. Don't miss **Gould's Secondhand Bookshop** at 32 King Street. This place is an experience in itself. Other interesting secondhand shops await at the southern end of Kings Street, beyond the railway station.

Leichhardt

Leichhardt can be reached by buses 440 and 445 from the QVB in the city. Map 1, p251

Although receiving less attention than the eccentricities of Glebe and Newtown, Leichhardt is a pleasant suburb, famous for its Italian connections and subsequently its eateries and cafés. Norton Street is the main focus. See eating and drinking, p153 for details.

Homebush Bay Olympic Park

Homebush Bay is about 14 km west of the city centre and is best reached by train (Western Line) from the city, or alternatively by Rivercat, from Circular Quay (Wharf 5) to Homebush Bay Wharf, from $20, child $10. The Olympic Explorer Bus is a convenient way to explore the site. It leaves every 15 mins between 0920-1700 daily from the VIC, Herb Elliot Ave, $10, children $5, T 131500. The Olympic Explorer links with the ferry services from Circular Quay. For tourist information see p33. Map 7, E3, p254

The centrepiece of a vast array of architecturally-stunning sports venues and public amenities, **Telstra Stadium** (formerly Stadium Australia) was the main focus of the games, being the venue for the opening and closing ceremonies, as well as track and field and soccer events. Although the Olympic flame has long been extinguished, it remains an important national venue for international and national rugby union, rugby league, Aussie rules football and soccer matches. Tours (45 minutes) are conducted hourly and daily from 1100-1500, adult $15.40, child $11.50. Next door is the state-of-the-art **Sydney Superdome** that hosted basketball and gymnastics during the games and now offers a huge indoor arena for a range of public events from music concerts to Australia's largest agricultural show, the Royal Easter Show. Guided tours available daily from 1000-1600.

Perhaps the most celebrated venue during the games was the **Sydney International Aquatic Centre** where the triumphant Aussie swimming team took on the world and won with such stars as Thorpe and Klim. The complex continues to hold international swimming and diving events and is now open to the public. Sydney Olympic Park has many other modern sports facilities including the State Sports, Sydney International Tennis, Hockey, Baseball and Archery Centres and is surrounded by superb parkland.

Bicentennial Park is a 100-hectare mix of dryland and conservation wetland and a popular spot for walking, jogging, birdwatching or simply feeding the ducks. Guided nature tours are available. Ask about the *Superpass* that allows multiple facility access and a complimentary swim from $34.90. Transportation by bus around Olympic Park and to/from the station is available from $2.20 point to point, $11per day.

● *The best view of the entire complex is from the observatory in the Novotel Hotel within the park.*

Parramatta

Can be reached by train direct from the city centre (Western Line) or bus route 520 from Circular Quay. The 50-min Parramatta Rivercat journey from Wharf 5 Circular Quay passes the Homebush Bay Olympic Park. The Parramatta Explorer Bus is a specialist service that explores the historical aspects of the city at weekends between 1000-1600. It stops at both the RiverCat terminal and the main railway station every 30 mins; $10, child $5, T 9630 3703. For tourist information see p34. Map 7, D2, p254

Often dubbed the city within the city, Parramatta is a culturally diverse centre and although its modern aesthetics are unremarkable, it does boast some of the nation's most historic sites. When the First Fleeters failed in their desperate attempts to grow crops in what is now Port Jackson in the city centre, they penetrated the upper reaches of the Parramatta River and established a farming settlement in 1788. Within three years the population had grown to over 100. The settlement was first known as Rose Hill before being renamed Parramatta – the name given to the area by the local Aboriginal tribe – the *Burramatta*. The oldest European site is **Elizabeth Farm**, 70 Alice Street, Rosehill, a 1793 colonial home-stead built for John and Elizabeth Macarthur, former pioneers in the Australian wool industry. It contains a number of interesting displays and is surrounded by a recreated 1830s garden.

Also of interest is the 1799 **Old Government House** in Parramatta Park. It is Australia's oldest public building and houses a fine collection of colonial furniture. Ghost tours are available every first and third Friday of the month from $22.

Experiment Farm Cottage, 9 Ruse Street, (closed Mondays) is the site of the colonial governments first land grant to former convict James Ruse in 1791. The cottage itself dates from 1834.

Parramatta River, which quietly glides past the city, is without doubt its most attractive natural attraction and it features in a number of heritage walking trails. These and many other historical details are displayed at the Parramatta Heritage and Visitors Information Centre.

Featherdale Wildlife Park

217 Kildare Rd, Doonside, **T** 9622 1644. *0900-1700 daily. $15, children $7.50, family $38. By car go via the M4 and turn off on to Reservoir Rd. After 4 km turn left on to Kildare Rd. Alternatively take the train from the city (Western Line) to Blacktown then bus 725 from the station* Map 7, D1, p254

The best wildlife park in the city beyond Taronga Zoo is Featherdale Wildlife Park in Doonside. It has the largest private collection of native Australian Wildlife in the country with over 2,000 animals on show. Unlike its all dominant competitor, Taronga Zoo in the city, many of its inhabitants, like the kookaburra and the enchanting tawny frogmouth (like a cross between a frog and an owl) roam free in the park, making themselves readily available for close inspection, photographs or a staring match. You can also hand feed kangaroos, wallabies and emus and cuddle a koala. The on-site shop is also excellent.

Australian Wildlife Park and Wonderland Sydney

Wallgrove Rd, Eastern Creek. **T** 9830 9100, www.wonderland.com.au *0900-1700 daily, Wildlife Park only $16.50, Wonderland $44, children $9.90 (Wonderland $29.70), family $47.50. Take the Wallgrove exit off the M4 westbound. Wonderlink is a transport and entry combo, **T** 131500. The Wonderland Express also offers transits from major hotels, **T** 9830 9187. Map 7, D1, p254*

Other face-to-face wildlife encounters can be had at The Australian Wildlife Park, part of Wonderland Sydney, a vast amusement park with many highly-staged aspects of Australiana from boomerang throwing to sheep mustering, as well as the usual vomit inducing thrill rides and inevitably tacky souvenir shops.

Penrith

T 4730 4333. Rafting sessions are now available to the public. Phone for details and directions. For tourist information, see p34. Map 8, F8, p255

Sitting at the base of the Blue Mountains and beside the Nepean River, Penrith offers a number of exciting water-based activities that have been augmented with the creation of the **Penrith**

Whitewater Stadium used as the canoe/kayak slalom venue for the 2000 Olympics. The **Sydney International Regatta Centre** has two purpose built facilities used for the rowing and canoeing events of the 2000 Olympics. Much more user friendly is the **Cables Waterski Park**, near the VIC, which offers cable-towed waterskiing, waterslides and pools.

City East: Kings Cross to Bondi

*East of the city sit some of Sydney's most intriguing and well-known suburbs, famous for their nightlife, architecture, gay communities and of course, their sublime urban beaches. The most famous (and notorious) suburb is **Kings Cross**, which still lures visitors by the score, all intent to revel in its seedy nightlife, or to secure a bed in its rash of lively backpackers. Many quite rightly find it highly over-rated and a major disappointment, soon waking (most probably with a mighty headache) to the realization that its true character goes little beyond the bottom of a beer glass. Fringing 'The Cross', the suburbs of **Darlinghurst**, **Surry Hills** and more recently, **Potts Point** and **Woolloomooloo**, all offer more substance, hosting some of the city's best contemporary dining. West of Darlinghurst, beyond **Oxford Street** (the undeniable focus of Sydney's overt gay community), is the attractive suburb of **Paddington**, where Victorian architecture provides the backdrop to some major parks, sporting venues and city attractions including the **Sydney Cricket Ground** (SCG) and **Fox Studios** in **Moore Park** and beyond that, the recreational pursuits on offer within the peaceful confines of **Centennial Park** (Sydney's largest). Further west, the whiff of salt air leads the way to the beachside suburbs of **Bondi**, **Bronte** and **Coogee** with **Bondi Beach** being world-famous for its enviably laid-back, quintessential Australian lifestyle.*

▶▶ *See Sleeping p128, Eating and drinking p156, Bars and clubs p173*

◉ Sights

Kings Cross

Reached by foot from the city via William St or Woolloomooloo or by bus, Sydney Explorer stop 9, Elizabeth Bay House stop 11, Woolloomooloo stop 13 (0840-1722 only) or regular bus services 311, 323-325, 327, 333. Or, by train on the Illawarra Line from Town Hall or Martin Pl. Between 2400 and 0430 Nightride buses replace trains, but check times and stops between 0600-2200, T 131500.
Map 3, B/C 11/12, p251

Even before arriving in Sydney you have probably heard of Kings Cross, the famous, if not notorious hub of Sydney nightlife and the long-established focus of sex, drugs and rock and roll. Situated near the navy's Woolloomooloo docks, the Cross has been a favourite haunt of visiting sailors and Sydneysiders for years.

Depending on your personality, age and life experience, you will either love or hate Kings Cross and it will be as good or as bad as you make it. It is hard to be indifferent. The main drag through the Cross is **Darlinghurst Road** which is the focus of the action, while Victoria Road is home to a rash of backpacker hostels. At the intersection of both and at the top of William Street, connecting the Cross with the city, is the huge and iconic Coca Cola sign. Although not obvious, drugs play a big part in Kings Cross, petty theft is common and intoxicated persons omnipresent. Always keep your wallet well under wraps. That said, Kings Cross is enormously popular with backpackers and Sydneysiders in general and it can provide a great (and often memorable) night out. It is also a great place to meet people, make contacts, find work, and even buy a car.

● *The best time to visit the Cross is in the small hours when the bars, the clubs and ladies of the night are all in full swing. In daylight it holds little appeal.*

Elizabeth Bay House

7 Onslow Ave, Elizabeth Bay, **T** 9356 3022. *Tue-Sun 1000-1630. $7, children $3, family $17. Map 3, A12, p251*

Amid its social mania there are a number of notable and more sedate sights in and around Kings Cross. Elizabeth Bay House is a revival-style estate that was built by popular architect John Verge for Colonial secretary Alexander Macleay in 1845. The interior is restored and faithfully furnished in accordance with the times and the house has a great outlook across the harbour.

Woolloomooloo

To the northwest of Kings Cross. Map 3, A10/11, p251

The delightfully named suburb of Woolloomooloo is the main east coast base for the Australian Navy and often, other visiting naval vessels that off-load their human cargos, which head immediately with obvious intent towards the souvenir shops of Kings Cross. Other than the warships and a scattering of lively pubs, it is the newly-developed **Woolloomooloo Wharf** and a pie-cart that are the major attractions. The new wharf has a clutch of fine restaurants that look over the marina towards the city and concentrate mainly on seafood. It is a popular dining alternative to the busy city centre and a great place to consider just what kind of job you must have to own a launch 'like that'.

● *If the wharf restaurants are beyond your budget, worry not, nearby is one of Sydney's best cheap eateries. Harry's Café de Wheels near the wharf entrance is something of an institution, selling its own $3 range of meat, mash, pea and gravy pies. The cart is open almost twenty four hours a day and has been for years.*

! 'Woolloomooloo' is thought to be derived from the Aboriginal word 'wulla mulla' meaning a male joey (young kangaroo).

Darlinghurst and Surry Hills

The area can be reached on foot from the city via William St, Liverpool St or Oxford St, or by buses 311-399. Map 3, p251

Both Darlinghurst and Surry Hills offer some great restaurants and cafés with Darlinghurst Road and Victoria Street, just south of Kings Cross, being the main focus. Here you will find some of Sydney's most popular eateries, consistently luring the crowds over from Kings Cross at night or providing a perfect lazy breakfast spot for the morning after. **Jewish Museum**, 148 Darlinghurst Road, *Sun to Thu 1000-1600, Fri 1000-1400, Sun 1100-1700, $10, children $6, family $22, tours available*, offers displays about the holocaust and history of Judaism in Australia from the arrival of the First Fleet in 1788.

Surry Hills is a mainly residential district and does not have quite the pizzaz of Darlinghurst, but it is well known for its traditional Aussie pubs that seem to dominate every street corner. One thing not to miss is the **Brett Whitley Museum and Gallery**, 2 Raper Street, *1000-1600 daily, $7*. The museum is the former studio and home of the late Brett, one of Sydney's most popular contemporary artists.

Paddington

Paddington can be reached by foot from the southeast corner of Hyde Park in the city via Oxford St. By buses 378-382 or the Bondi and Bay Explorer from Circular Quay and Railway Square. Map 3, F/H12, p251, See also p211

The big attraction in Paddington is **Oxford Street**, which stretches east from the city and southwest corner of Hyde Park to the northwest corner of Centennial Park and Bondi Junction. The city end of Oxford Street surrounding Taylor Square is one of the most happening areas of the city with cheap eateries, cafés, restaurants, clubs and bars. It is also a major focus for the city's gay community. Then, as Oxford street heads west into Paddington proper it becomes lined with boutique clothes shops, art shops and bookshops, cafés and a number of good pubs. Many people coincide a visit to Oxford Street with the colourful **Paddington Market**, held every Saturday from 1000.

Behind Oxford Street, heading north, are leafy suburbs with small, tightly-packed, Victorian terrace houses, interspersed with **art galleries** and old pubs, all hallmarks of Paddington. For a full listing of galleries pick up a free *Art Find* brochure from one of the galleries or the Sydney VIC. A stroll down Glenmore Road to the cross roads of Goodhope and Heeley Street will reveal some of the best of them.

South of Oxford Street is the old Georgian **Victoria Barracks** which has been a base for British and Australian Army battalions since 1848. It remains fully functional and visitors are welcome to see a flag-raising ceremony, a marching band performance and to join a guided tour on Thursdays at 1000. There is also a small museum, *Thu 1000-1400 Sun (museum only) 1000-1500, free*.

Just to the south of the Barracks in **Moore Park** and in stark contrast, is the famous **Sydney Cricket Ground (SCG)** and next-door the **Sydney Football Stadium (SFS)**. The hallowed arena of the SCG is a place of worship for many enthusiasts of Australia's national sport. In winter the SCG is taken over by the *Sydney Swans*, Australian-rules football team, which has a local, though no less fanatical following. The Sydney Football Stadium was for many years the focus of major national and international rugby union, league and soccer matches, but it now plays second fiddle to the mighty (and far less atmospheric) Telstra Stadium in Homebush. Tours of both stadiums are available to the public, **T** 9380 0383. *Bondi Explorer Bus* stop 16. See also Sports, p203.

Also within Moore Park are the $300 million **Fox Studios**, Lang Road, **T** 9383 4333, www.foxstudios.com.au, *1000-2200, daily, free*, which opened in 1999. They have been used in the filming of such recent blockbusters as *Mission Impossible II*, *Matrix II* and the

Star Wars trilogy. Parts of the complex are open to the public and host a fairly unremarkable range of attractions including cinemas, shops, restaurants and markets.

Just to the east of the Fox Studios Complex is **Centennial Park**, which at 220 hectares is Sydney's largest. It provides a vast arena for walking, cycling, horse-riding, roller-blading and bird-watching. The **Parklands Sports Centre** also provides tennis, roller-hockey and basketball, **T** 9662 7033. In late summer there is a nightly outdoor **Moonlight Cinema** programme, that often showcases old classics like *Monty Python* and *ET*. The park can be accessed from the north-west corner (Oxford Street) and Randwick to the south (Alison Rd). For general park information **T** 9339 6699, www.cp.nsw.gov.au *Bondi and Bay Explorer Bus*, stop 14.

Watsons Bay

Watsons Bay is reached by ferry from Circular Quay Wharfs 2 and 4, or by buses 342 and 325 from Circular Quay. Map 1, p251

Watsons Bay, sitting on the leeward side of **South Head** that guards the mouth of Sydney Harbour, provides an ideal city escape and is best reached by ferry from Circular Quay. As well as being home to one of Sydney's oldest and most famous seafood restaurants – Doyles (see p162) – it offers some quiet coves, attractive swimming beaches and peninsula walks. The best beaches are to be found at **Camp Cove** about a 10-minute walk north of the ferry terminal. A little further north is **Lady Bay Beach**, a secluded and popular naturist beach. The best walk in the area is the one- to two-hour jaunt to the 1858 **Hornby Lighthouse** and South Head itself, then south to the **HMAS Watson Naval Chapel** and the area known as **The Gap**. The clifftop aspect provides greats views out towards the ocean and north to North Head and Manly.

The area also boasts some interesting historical sites. Camp Cove was used by Governor Phillip, commander of the *First Fleet*, as an

overnight stop before reaching Port Jackson in the Inner Harbour.
Vaucluse House, Wentworth Road, Vaucluse, south of Watson's
Bay, **T** 9388 7922, *Tue-Sun 1000-1630, $7, children $3, family $17.*
Was built in 1827 and is a fine example of an early colonial estate. It
is furbished in period style and has a gift shop and tearooms.

Southern Beaches: Bondi, Bronte, Clovelly and Coogee

*Bondi can be reached by car from the city, via Oxford Street, or by bus
on the* Bondi and Bay Explorer *or services 321, 322, 365, 366 and 380.
By rail first get to Bondi Junction (Illawara Line) then take the bus
(numbers above). Coogee is serviced by buses 372-374 and
314-315.* Map 6, p253

Bondi Beach is by far the most famous of Sydney's many ocean
beaches. Its hugely inviting stretch of sand is a prime venue for
surfing, swimming and sunbathing – the epitome of Sydney's
lifestyle. Behind the beach, Bondi's bustling waterfront and village
offers a tourist trap of cafés, restaurants, bars, surf and souvenir
shops. People-watching in Bondi is almost as entertaining as its
beach activities. For years Bondi has been a popular suburb for
alternative lifestylers and visiting backpackers keen to avoid the
central city. It is also the place to see or be seen. You will encounter
everything from the tanned and the torso inflated to the scantily
clad and the silicone implanted. However, having said that, if
solitude and nature is your thing, then you can still find it on Bondi
Beach. At dawn, when the sun creeps above the ocean, throwing
only the occasional shadow of a local and his dog down the beach to
meet your own, it can be hard to imagine it becoming like a set from
Baywatch once the sun turns on the heat. If you intend swimming at
Bondi bear in mind, that, like many Australian beaches it is subject to
dangerous rips so always swim between the yellow and red flags,
clearly marked on the beach. Watchful lifeguards, also clad in yellow
and red, are on hand for advice, or at worst, to pluck you from the
surf if you get in to difficulty. Bondi Beach is the focus of wild

celebrations on Christmas Day with one huge beach party, usually culminating in a mass dash naked into the sea.

To the south of Bondi Beach, and best reached by a coastal walkway connecting Bondi to Coogee (one of the most popular walks in the city), is the small oceanside suburb of **Bronte**. This little enclave offers a smaller, quieter and equally attractive beach with a number of very popular **cafés** frequented especially at the weekend for brunch.

A little further south still is **Clovelly**, which has another sheltered beach especially good for kids. Many people finish their walk at **Coogee**, which is not only in possession of a silly name but a fine beach and a bustling waterfront, full of the usual cafés, restaurants and novelty shops. Although playing second fiddle to Bondi, it is also a popular haunt for backpackers or couples keen to stay near the beach and outside the city centre.

City North: Manly to the Northern Beaches

*Immediately north of the harbour bridge is **North Sydney**, a corporate sub-forest of neon-clad high rises. The weekday haunt of the business suit there is little to entertain the visitor here except the glimpse of the odd outrageously loud tie, a few good restaurants and another cornucopia of stunning views towards the city. Just to the east is the surprisingly quiet and leafy suburb of **Kirribilli**, home to Kirribilli House – the Prime Minister's Sydney residence – a property that most Sydneysiders would argue possesses architecture and a garden with more character and colour than Australia's most recent Prime Ministers, or indeed his phlegmatic Canberra colleagues.*

> **!** The name 'Coogee' is thought to be derived from the Aboriginal word meaning 'smelly seaweed'. Contrary to the name, you will find the beach largely odourless.

Further east, fringed by charming harbour bays replete with expensive yachts and some of the most enviable real estate in Australia, are the well-to-do suburbs of **Cremorne**, **Mossman** and **Balmoral**. Amidst all this haughtiness the largest and best area of prime real estate is actually given over to the world-famous **Taronga Zoo** and (amongst its many other tenants) a troupe of monkeys picking each other's spots and behaving with enchanting delinquency.

North Head, with its magnificent city views guards the harbour entrance and, like a suburban necklace around it, **Manly** thrives as a beach resort within the city, attracting thousands of visitors who issue forth from the Circular Quay ferry already abuzz with the scenic harbour trip.

North of Manly, a string of magnificent beaches and beachside communities including Dee Why, Collaroy, Mona Vale, Avalon and Palm Beach all combine to form the city's **Northern Beaches**, providing excellent swimming and surfing.

▸▸ See Sleeping p136 and Eating and drinking p163

 Sights

North Sydney and surrounds
Map 1, p251

On the northern side of the Harbour Bridge a small stand of high-rise buildings with neon signs heralds the mainly commercial suburb of North Sydney. There is little here for the tourist to justify a special visit, but nearby, the suburb of **McMahons Point** and more especially **Milsons Point**, directly below the bridge, both offer fine city views.

Blues Point Reserve, on the shores of Lavender Bay, offer the best city views in McMahons Point. It can be reached via Blues Point Road which in itself boasts a number of fine cafés. If you are

Sydney

87

short for time the best vantage point is without doubt right below the bridge at Milsons Point. There is a lookout point which looks straight across to Circular Quay and the Opera House almost in the shadow of the bridge. Few realize they are standing right above the speeding traffic in the harbour tunnel below. Milsons Point is also home to the seldom-used **Luna Park**, a former fun park complete with colourful ferris wheel, that even in its haunting silence has become another icon of the inner harbour. A huge smiling face that once beamed across to the city centre from its facade, has now been moved to the Powerhouse Museum near Darling Harbour. Another attraction is the old **Sydney Olympic Pool** next door, offering more spectacular city views.

Kirribilli is a serene little suburb that lies directly to the east of the bridge. **Admiralty House** and **Kirribilli House**, the Sydney residences of the Governor General and the Prime Minister sit overlooking the Opera House on Kirribilli Point. Both are closed to the public and are best seen from the water. Beyond Kirribilli, are the congenial residential suburbs and secluded bays of **Neutral Bay** and **Cremorne**.

● *At night, the ferry trip across the harbour to the city from Cremorne Wharf is almost worth the journey in itself.*

Mosman and Balmoral
Mosman is best reached by ferry from Circular Quay (Wharf 4) to the Mosman Bay where a bus awaits to take you up the hill to the commercial centre. Alternatively take buses 238, 250 or for Mosman and the zoo 247 from Wynyard Station in the CBD . Map 1, p251

Mosman possesses a very pleasant village feel of which its well-to-do residents are rightly proud. Situated so close to the city centre, yet almost like an island, it has developed in to one of the most exclusive and expensive areas of real estate in the city. However, don't let this put you off. Mosman, in unison with its equally comfy, neighbouring, beachside suburb of Balmoral, are both great escapes by ferry from the city centre and offer some fine eateries, designer clothes shops, walks and beaches, plus one of Sydney's must-see attractions, Sydney's Taronga Zoo (see below).

★ Taronga Zoo

Bradley's Head Rd, **T** 9969 2777, tours **T** 9969 2455, www.zoo.nsw.gov.au *0900-1700 daily. Zoo $23, children $12, family $57. Taronga is best reached by ferry from Circular Quay (Wharf 2). Ferries every half-hour Mon-Fri 0715-1845, Sat 0845-1845 and Sun 0845-1730. A Zoo Pass combo ticket which includes ferry transfers and zoo entry costs $28.40, child $14.30. Map 1, p251*

This world-famous, government-run establishment was first created in 1881 in the grounds of Moore Park, south of Centennial Park, Paddington, before being relocated to Bradley's Head, Mosman in 1916. It has an extensive collection of native Australian species, including the obligatory koala, platypus and marsupials, to add to a particularly impressive collection of colourful Australian birds. All the usual suspects are also in residence, including gorilla, tiger, elephant, bear, giraffe and the largest captive troupe of chimps in the world. Their antics alone will keep you spellbound and giggling for hours. One of the added attractions of Taronga is its position in relation to the city and its views. You will almost certainly need a full day to explore the various exhibits on offer and there are plenty of events staged throughout the day to keep both adults and children entertained. The best of these is the **Kodak Bird Show** which is staged twice daily in an open-air arena overlooking the city. Don't forget your camera and be prepared to duck. Taronga is built on a hill so you are recommended to take the awaiting bus from the zoo wharf up to the main entrance then work your way back down to the lower gate. Alternatively, for a small additional charge on entry, you can take a scenic gondola ride to the main gate. If you are especially interested in wildlife it pays to check out the dynamic programme of specialist public tours on offer. The **Night Zoo** tour after hours is especially popular.

North Shore walks and beaches
Map 1, p251

Balmoral Beach is one of the most popular and sheltered in the harbour. Other than the obvious attractions it offers for those foreigners from colder climbs, it is the scene of quite a bizarre spectacle just after dawn – here, perhaps more than anywhere else in the city, you will observe Sydneysiders enjoying something that is quintessentially Australian: the early morning, pre-work dip. From about 0630 it seems as if half the resident population turn out for their habitual morning constitutional or swim. If you don't fancy being so healthy, you can always hide in one of the beachside cafés, order a full cooked breakfast and a double espresso, light up a cigarette and watch.

Balmoral Beach overlooks **Middle Harbour** whose waters infiltrate far in to suburbs of the North Shore.

On **Middle Head**, jutting out in to the harbour beyond Mosman, you will find one of Sydney's best and most secluded naturist beaches, **Cobblers Beach**. Access is via a little-known track behind the softball pitch near the end of Military Road. The atmosphere is friendly and congenial and the crowd truly cosmopolitan. However, unless you are gay and looking for a wild time, avoid the peninsula on the eastern edge of the beach. The beach is served several times a day by a refreshments boat that stocks soft drinks and ice cream. The only problem may be working out where to put your change

Clothed again, you might like to amble along to the tip of

! Bradley's Head was the temporary site of the evil terrorist's house in the film *Mission Impossible II* (2000).

Middle Head where some old wartime fortifications look out across North Head and the harbour entrance, or enjoy the walk to the tip of **Bradley's Head**, below the zoo, with its wonderful views of the city. Park your car at the Ashton Park car park about a kilometre before the zoo wharf and find the track to the west that skirts around the water's edge. Alternatively, just follow the path, east from the zoo's lower entrance. The NSW National Parks and Wildlife Service offer guided tours to Bradley's Head on the first and third Sunday of each month at 1330-1530 and to Middle Head on the second and fourth Sunday of the month from 1030-1230, $13.20, children $9.90.

Manly
*The best way to reach Manly is by ferry from Circular Quay (wharfs 2 and 3). The standard ferries cost $5, children $2.50, taking 30 mins while the Jet Cat takes 15 mins, $6.30. Both leave on a regular basis daily. Alternatively take bus 151 or 171 from Wynyard in the city, **T** 131500. Map 5, p253*

Manly is by far the most visited suburb on the North Shore, and for many visitors serves as a self-contained holiday resort, offering an oceanside sanctuary away from the manic city centre. The heart of the community sits on the neck of the **North Head** peninsula, which guards the entrance of Sydney Harbour. **Manly Beach**, which fringes the ocean or eastern edge of the suburb, is very much the main attraction. At its southern end an attractive oceanside walkway connects Manly Beach with two smaller, quieter alternatives, **Fairy Bower Beach** and **Shelly Beach**.

As you might expect, Manly comes with all the tourist trappings, including an attractive tree-lined waterfront, fringed with cafés, restaurants, souvenir and surf shops, that complements its wealth of accommodation options. Connecting Manly Beach with the ferry terminal and **Manly Cove**, on the western or harbour side, is the **Corso**, a fairly tacky pedestrian

Beachlife

Manly Beach is one of Sydney's most popular, sandwiching the suburb between Pacific surf on one side and the calmer waters of the Harbour on the other.

precinct lined with cheap eateries, bars and souvenir shops. Its only saving grace is the **market** which is held at its eastern end every weekend. Just to the west of the ferry terminal is West Esplanade which prides itself in a quiet swimming beach (with shark net), ideal for kids. At the western end, next-door to one another but with sharply contrasting contents, are **Oceanworld** and the **Manly Art Gallery and Museum**.

Oceanworld

West Esplanade, **T** 9949 2644,
www.oceanworldmanly.com   *1000-1730 daily. $16, children $8, family $25. Regular tours are available. The sharks are fed Mon, Wed and Fri at 1100.*
Map 6, D/E1, p253

Oceanworld is a long-established aquarium that, although it can't compete with Sydney Aquarium in the Darling Harbour, is still worth a wander, especially with children. Its star attractions are its sharks, which play a leading role in its emphasis on 'dangerous' Australian creatures. Not all its charges are aquatic: snakes, spiders and scorpions are also on show.

Manly Art Gallery and Museum

West Esplanade, **T** 9949 1776.   *Tue-Sun 1000-1700. $3.50, children $1.10.   Map 6, D1, p253*

Manly Art Gallery and Museum showcases an interesting array of permanent historical items with the obvious emphasis on all things 'beach', while the gallery offers both permanent and temporary shows of contemporary art and photography. Given the price of entry it is well worth a look. The Manly Art Gallery and Museum also hosts the Manly Arts Festival (see Festivals, p191).

North Head and The Quarantine Station

T 9247 5033. *Tours Mon, Wed, Frid, Sat and Sun at 1310, $11, children $7.70. Popular daily 3-hour Ghost Tour includes supper, 1930 Wed $22.50, Fri-Sun $27.50. A 2-hour kids version at 1830 is also available, $13.20. Bookings recommended. Scenic Drive (bus 135 from Manly wharf). Map 1, p251*

The tip of **North Head**, to the south of Manly, is worth a visit, if only to soak up the views across the harbour and out to sea. The cityscape is especially stunning at dawn. Just follow Scenic Drive to the very end. The **Quarantine Station**, which takes up a large portion of the peninsula, was used from 1832 to harbour ships known to be carrying diseases like smallpox, bubonic plague, cholera and Spanish influenza, and to protect the new colony from the spread of such nasties. The station closed in 1984 and is now administered by the NSW National Parks and Wildlife Service.

Although it is closed to the public, the **Sydney Water Pollution Control Station**, on the peninsula's northeastern corner, is worth a mention. It must be the only place in the world with a street called *Poo Avenue* and more importantly, is one of the last remaining Sydney strongholds of the long-nosed bandicoot, an eternally appealing, rat-sized marsupial, that once thrived throughout the region.

Manly offers a wealth of other activities including cycling, sea kayaking, roller-blading, diving and of course surfing. The VIC lists outlets and hire prices. Manly also hosts a major **Jazz Festival** in October and a **Food and Wine Festival** in June.

The 10-km **Manly Scenic Walkway**, from Manly to Spit Bridge, is an excellent scenic harbour walk. It starts from the end of West Esplanade and takes around three to four hours. You can catch a 144 or 143 bus back to Manly from the Spit. Before you attempt this walk try to get hold of the NSW Parks and Wildlife Service *Manly Scenic Walkway* leaflet from the Sydney or Manly VICs or Sydney Harbour National Parks Office, Cadman's Cottage, The Rocks, **T** 9247 5033.

Northern Beaches

The free Northern Beaches Visitors Guide, *available from the Sydney VIC is an excellent information booklet covering just about everything from accommodation to shopping, anywhere north of Manly to Barrenjoey Head, www.sydneynorthernbeaches.com.au The L90 bus from Wynard in the city goes via all the main northen beach suburbs to Palm Beach. It leaves every 30 mins daily. Map 7, A-D6, p254*

The coast north of Manly is inundated with bays and fine beaches that stretch 10 km to **Barrenjoey Head** at Broken Bay and the entrance to the Hawkesbury River harbour. Perhaps the most popular of these are **Narrabeen**, **Avalon** and **Whale Beach,** but there are many to choose from. Narabeen has the added attraction of a large lake that is used for sailing, canoeing and windsurfing, while Avalon and Whale Beach, further north, are smaller, quite picturesque and more sheltered. A day trip to the very tip of Barrenjoey Head is recommended.

The most popular walk in the area is to the summit of Barrenjoey Head and the historic **lighthouse**, built in 1881. The views both north and south are spectacular. Access is from the Barrenjoey Boathouse car park and via the northern end of Station Beach. The area is complemented by **Palm Beach**, a popular Sydney weekend getaway, with some fine restaurants and, of course, another great beach. Palm Beach has been made especially famous by the vacuous Aussie soap opera *Home and Away* with much of the filming taking place on the beach.

There are many water activities on offer in the area focused mainly on **Pittwater**, a large bay on the sheltered western side of the peninsula. Day cruises up the **Hawkesbury River**, *$30,* *children $15*, or shorter excursions to **The Basin**, which has pretty beaches and camping areas in the Ku-ring-gai Chase National Park, are also available from the Palm Beach public wharf, **T** 9997 4815.

The **Barrenjoey Boathouse** has boats and kayaks for hire, **T** 9974 4229 and a Dive Centre, **T** 9974 4261. If you are particularly flush you can even fly in to Pittwater from Sydney harbour by **floatplane**, **T** 1300 656 787, www.sydneybyseaplane.com

Listings

● Museums and galleries

- **Aboriginal and Tribal Art Centre** Art and artefacts, p195.
- **Art Gallery of New South Wales** Notable collection of local, national, Aboriginal, Asian and European fine art, p61.
- **Australian Museum** City's principal natural history museum: fauna, flora, geology and indigenous history, p59.
- **Brett Whitley Museum and Gallery** Diverse work of one of Sydney's most famous and popular contemporary artists, p82.
- **Coo-ee Emporium and Aboriginal Art Gallery** Authentic Aboriginal arts, crafts and artefacts, p195.
- **Jewish Museum** Judaism in Australia from 1788, p82.
- **Justice and Police Museum** Small legal and police museum set in the original Police Court buildings, p44.
- **Ken Done Gallery** One of Sydney's most popular, prolific and highly colourful contemporary artists, p198.
- **Ken Duncan Gallery** The work of one of Australia's finest landscape photographers, p202.
- **Manly Art Gallery and Museum** Permanent and temporary shows of contemporary art and photography, p94.
- **Museum Of Contemporary Art** Modern art, photography and Aboriginal works from recent decades, p45.
- **Museum of Sydney** First settlement to the modern day, p52.
- **National Maritime Museum** Permanent and temporary exhibitions of Australia's complex maritime history, p63.
- **Peter Lik Gallery** Landscape photographer, p202.
- **Powerhouse Museum** Diverse and innovative, p68.
- **Rocks Toy Museum** 3,000 toys from the last 200 years, p217.
- **SH Ervin Gallery** Host to historical art exhibitions, p49.
- For listings of the many **commercial galleries** in Paddington, get a free *Art Find* brochure from galleries or the Sydney VIC.

Blue Mountains 101

Congenial townships, stunning lookouts, a range of bush walks, precipitous waterfalls and, for once in Australia, the welcome hint of seasons.

Hawkesbury River Region 113

Bounding the city to the northwest, one of the state's longest and most significant waterways makes a peaceful and rural day trip.

Ku-ring-gai Chase National Park 114

At the northern end of the voluminous city, Ku-ring-gai Chase sits like a great green book end. Rugged sandstone country and Aboriginal rock art.

Royal National Park 115

Australia's oldest national park, easily accessible from the city and in recent years scorched annually by bush fires. Shades of black and green, fringed by sandy beaches, coastal walks and ocean views.

Botany Bay National Park 117

Like some highlighted historical manuscript, the site of Captain Cook's first landing in April 1770. Unchanged vistas of the ocean on one side and the hum of the vast modern city on the other.

Blue Mountains

The 'Blueys', as they are affectionately known, form part of the Great Dividing Range, 70 km, or two hours, west of Sydney, and contain no less than five national parks covering a total area of 10,000 sq-km. Although just as impressive, they are not really mountains, but a network of eroded river valleys, gorges and bluffs, that have formed over millions of years. The result is a huge wonderland of natural features, from precipitous cliffs to dramatic waterfalls and canyons, not to mention the most dramatic limestone caves on the continent.

Although once the happy home of the Daruk Aboriginals, the Blue Mountains were initially seen by the first Europeans as a highly inconvenient barrier to whatever could be plundered on the other side. Incredibly, for almost a quarter of a century, they remained that way, before finally being traversed in 1813 by explorers Blaxland, Wentworth and Lawson. To this day the impenetrable geography still limits transportation with essentially the same two convict-built roads and railway line, completed over a century ago, reaching west through a string of settlements from Glenbrook to Lithgow. Merely passing through you are almost unaware of the dramatic precipices, canyons and viewpoints that exist at the end of almost every other street or cul-de-sac.

For decades the Blue Mountains have been a favourite weekend or retirement destination for modern-day Sydney escapees, who welcome the distinctly cooler temperatures and the colourful seasons that the extra elevation creates. Beauty and climate aside, the Blue Mountains also present some excellent walking opportunities, as well as other more fearsome activities like abseiling, canyoning and rock climbing. Given the region's popularity there are also a glut of good restaurants and a wide range of accommodation options from showpiece backpackers to romantic hideaways.

▸ See Sleeping p140, Eating and drinking p165 and Transport p32

⊙ Sights

Glenbrook
74 km from Sydney. For tourist information see p37. *Map 8, F8, p255*

Proud of its European roots and its railway heritage, the pretty village of Glenbrook, just beyond the **Nepean River**, acts as the unofficial gateway to the Blue Mountains. Fringing the village, south of the highway, is the southern section of the **Blue Mountains National Park** and access to numerous attractions, including the **Red Hands Cave**, a fine example of Aboriginal rock art. The distinctive hand stencils made on the cave wall are thought to be over 1,600 years old and were made by blowing ochre from the mouth. You can reach the caves either by road or by foot (8 km in total there and back) from the Glenbrook Creek causeway, just beyond the park entrance.

There are also shorter walks to the **Jellybean Pool**, that does the shape of the confection proud, and the **Euroka Clearing,** a basic NPWS campsite and the ideal spot to see grey kangaroos, especially early or late in the day. For a map of the park and its attractions call in at the Glenbrook VIC (see p37). To reach the park gate ($5 day-use, walkers free), take Ross Rd behind the VIC on to Burfitt Pde and then follow Bruce Road.

The lookouts at **The Bluff**, at the end of Brook Road (slightly further east off Burfitt, then Grey), are also worth a look and provide a taste of even better things to come. North of the highway in Glenbrook you can also follow signs to the **Lennox Bridge**,the oldest in Australia, built by convicts in 1833. Nearby, in **Knapsack Park**, the Marge's and Elizabeth Lookouts provide great views back towards Sydney's western suburbs.

Beyond Blaxland and Springwood is the small settlement of **Faulconbridge**, home to the **Norman Lindsay Gallery and Museum**. Lindsay (1879-1969) is just one of many noted artists that have found the Blue Mountains conducive to their creativity. He was particularly well known for his depictions of female nudes, which at the time caused more than a little controversy. In contrast, his children's book *The Magic Pudding* (1918) is an Australian classic. His studio, 14 Norman Lindsay Crescent, *1000-1600 daily, $8, child $4,* (if not his models) remains very much the way he left it.

Wentworth Falls
113 km from Sydney. Map 8, F4, p255

For most, it is the stunning **lookouts** across **Wentworth Falls** and the **Jamieson Valley** that offer the first memorable introduction to the dramatic, precipitous and spacious scenery of the Blue Mountains. But don't count on it. Sometimes, when the clouds are intent on meeting you personally, the experience can be little more than an unremarkable view of a car park and a rather sexy ice-cream van. However, supposing the weather is conducive, the same car park heralds the start of some superb walking tracks that take in viewpoints around the falls and some mighty precipitous sections down to their base. The best is the four-hour **Wentworth Pass Walk** that crosses the top of the falls, and then descends precariously down to the valley floor. The track then skirts the cliff base, through rainforest, before climbing back up via the dramatic **Valley of the Waters** gorge to the **Conservation Hut** (see below). There you can reward yourself with a good coffee before completing the adventure with an easy walk back to the car park. Another alternative is the five-hour **National Pass Walk** that quite remarkably follows a cutting halfway up the cliff, miraculously carved out in the 1890s. Both walks are hard and certainly not for sufferers of vertigo, involving steep sections

! The 'blue' label derives from the visual effects of sunlight on oils released by the cloak of gum trees that liberally swathe the valleys and plateaus.

around cliff edges and laddered sections, but if you are able, either one is highly recommended. Give yourself plenty of time and make sure you get maps from the Conservation Hut before setting out. The base section of the Wentworth Pass can be a little vague at times, though some improvements are being made to both tracks. Go prepared and don't forget your camera. If you are short of time, or are looking for something less demanding, try the **Den Fenella Track**, which will take you to some good lookouts, you can then return or (preferably) keep going west to the Conservation Hut along the **Overcliff Track**. Better still is the magical **Undercliff Track** to **Princes Rock Lookout**.

Leura
119 km west of Sydney. Map 8, E3, p255

Although the pretty village of Leura plays second fiddle to Katoomba, the two essentially merge. Possessing a distinct air of elegance, the residents of Leura are proud of their village and in particular their gardens which change colourfully with the seasons. **Everglades Gardens**, 37 Everglades Avenue, *1000-1700 daily, $6, child $2*, provide the best horticultural showpiece and have done since the early 1930s.

The **Mall** forms the main thoroughfare and it is replete with interesting shops, cafés and restaurants. The **Candy Store** in the Strand Arcade will send anyone with a sweet tooth in to a veritable frenzy, while **Megalong Books** on the Mall is the place to go for Blue Mountains books and maps. If you have kids in tow, or have an interest in toys and railways, then the **Leuralla and NSW Toy and Railway Museum** on Olympian Parade, *1000-1700 daily, $6, child $2*, is well worth a look, hosting lots of the old favourites including Noddy, Action Man and Barbie, as well as train sets and memorabilia galore.

A short stroll west of the museum is the **Gordon Falls Lookout**, which is worth a look. There are several other walks and lookouts around the cliff fringes in Leura with the best being the short 500-m walk to the aptly named **Sublime Lookout**. Reached alongside the equally sublime golf course on Watkins Road, this viewpoint offers arguably the best view of the **Jamieson Valley** and **Mount Solitary**. Follow signs from Gladstone Road, west of The Mall.

Katoomba and around

122 km west of Sydney. For tourist information, see p37.
Map 8, E3, p255

Considered the capital of the Blue Mountains, the historic town of Katoomba offers an interesting mix of old and new and a truly cosmopolitan ambience, attesting to its development over the decades from a small mining village and well-to-do tourist destination, to a bustling commercial conglomerate. As well as the wealth of amenities and activities based in the town many come here simply to see the archetypal, two-dimensional postcard image of the Blue Mountains transformed in to the real thing from the famous **Three Sisters** lookout at Echo Point.

A steady stream of tourist traffic floods relentlessly down Katoomba's main drag towards **Echo Point** where cascades of sightseers and babbles of 'Oohs' and 'Aghhs' celebrate the Blue Mountains' most famous vista – the **Three Sisters**. Like the golden ramparts of some grandiose tectonic castle they offer the perfect glowing foreground to the expansive backdrop of the forested **Jamieson Valley** and the distant sandstone bluffs of **Mount Solitary**. It is little wonder the place is so popular, since here you can see the Blue Mountains' grandeur and their colour in a scene that seems ever changing with the weather and the light. Built precariously 170 m above the valley floor the lookout seems to defy gravity. The only low point is of course the crowds that come and go as if on a mission. Given that, dawn and sunset are far better times to visit, and in the evening the stacks are spotlit.

Strangely, however, after the spectacle in sunlight, this is quite disappointing. From the lookout it is possible to walk around to the stacks and descend the taxing **Giant Stairway Walk** (half an hour) to the valley floor. From there you join the **Federal Pass Track**, back through the forest below the cliffs to the **Katoomba Cascades** and **Orphan Rock**. As the name suggests it is a single pillar that became separated from the nearby cliff over many centuries of erosion. From Orphan Rock it is a short walk to a choice of exits – the hard option, on foot, up the 1000-step **Furbers Steps**, or for the less adventurous, the **Scenic Railway**. Give yourself three hours for the complete circuit.

Katoomba presents many other excellent walking options, including the **Narrow Neck Plateau** (variable times) and **The Ruined Castle** (12 km, seven hours). The latter starts from the base of the Scenic Railway and can be made as part of an extended overnight trip to the summit of **Mount Solitary**. Recommended, but go prepared. The **Grand Canyon** walk is 5-km long and takes four hours. Leaving from Neates Glen, through Evans Lookout Road and Blackheath, it is also a cracker.

West of Echo Point the junction of Cliff Drive and Violet Street will deliver you to the highly commercial **Scenic World**, with its trilogy of unusual scenic transportation and insidious attempts to make you revisit your breakfast. The **Scenic Railway** option takes you on an exhilarating descent to the valley floor on what is reputed to be the world's steepest 'inclined funicular railway'. It's essentially a hairy 415-m tandem skydive in a tram. At the bottom you can take a boardwalk through the forest to see an **old coal mine** with an audio-visual display and bronze sculpture, or alternatively disappear discreetly into the woods to be violently sick. In contrast, the **Scenic Skyway** option at least keeps the angles and nerves within the realms of worldly physics and biochemistry, as well as providing an oh-so-pleasant bird's-eye view of the valley floor and the surrounding cliffs. The last in the trio, and the latest addition, is the modern **Scenicscender**, which is essentially like a combination of the two. If you survive that there is also a **cinema** showing a Blue Mountains documentary on demand and a revolving restaurant, which no doubt is their last gasp effort to see you on your way with an empty stomach. Contact details are **T** 4782 2699, www.scenicworld.com.au *0900-1700 daily, Railway and Scenicsender $12, one way $6, Skyway $10*.

Maxvision Edge Cinema, 225 Great Western Highway, shows new release films in the evening. Its six-storey, 18 m-high, 24 m-wide screen, offers an action-packed and distinctly precipitous film of the Blue Mountains. Of more environmental and historical interest is the segment about the **Polemic Pine**, an entirely new but senescent species that was discovered in the deepest wilderness areas of the **Wollemi National Park**, apparently causing an almost audible stir within the world's botanical community, as well as from the young fellow who found it.

Walking, rock-climbing, canyoning, mountain biking and abseiling are the five major activities in the Blue Mountains and several Katoomba-based operators offer supervised package deals. Other options include horse riding, 4WD adventures and numerous day tours to attractions like the **Jenolan Caves** or the stunning **Kanangra-Boyd National Park**. The VIC (see p37) has full listings.

Medlow Bath, Blackheath and Mount Victoria
126 km west of Sydney Map 8, E2/C2, p255

From Katoomba the Great Western Highway heads north through the pretty villages of Medlow Bath, Blackheath and Mount Victoria. Although not as commercial as their bustling neighbour, all provide excellent accommodation, restaurants and are fringed both north and south by equally stunning views and excellent walks. To the west is the easily accessible **Megalong Valley**, particularly well known for its horse trekking, while to the east, in contrast, is the **Grose Valley**, largely inaccessible stunner and the great barrier to many an early Sydney explorer. The **Evans** and

Govetts Leap lookouts east of Blackheath provide the best easily accessible viewpoints, but there are also some lesser-known spots well worth a visit.

In **Medlow Bath**, nature's architecture gives way momentarily to the human form, with the historic Hydro Majestic Hotel. Built in 1903 it was, at the time, the longest building in Australia and, given its cliff-top position, could also boast some of the most beautiful views. Though a hotel in its own right, its original, primary function, was as a sanatorium, offering all manner of health therapies, from mud baths to spas, not to mention 'the strict abstinence from alcohol'. At the time the rarefied air in the Blue Mountains was hailed as a remedy all for all city ills and people flocked to the Hydro to 'take the cure'. Today, although the mud baths (and thankfully the prohibition) have gone, the hotel still provides fine accommodation and a great spot for afternoon tea (or indeed a small libation).

Blackheath is a sleepy little village with an atmosphere enhanced in autumn when the trees take on golden hues. There are two lookouts well worth visiting. The first, Evans Lookout, is accessed east along Evans Lookout Road (funny that) and provides the first of many viewpoints across the huge and dramatic expanse of the Grose Valley. One of the best walks in the region, The Grand Canyon Trail, departs from Neates Glen, off Evans Lookout Rd (5 km, five hours). From there you descend down through the rainforest and follow Greaves Creek through moss-covered rock tunnels and overhangs, before climbing back up to Evans Lookout. The other lookout, Govetts Leap, is stunning and has the added attraction of the Bridal Veil Falls, the highest – but not necessarily the most dramatic – in the Blue Mountains. It is certainly a memorable view and one Charles Darwin once described in 1836 as 'stupendous'. Just before the lookout car park is the NPWS Heritage Centre, which is worth a visit providing up-to-date walks information, maps, guides and gifts (see p37). The Fairfax Heritage Track, built to accommodate wheelchairs, links the centre with the lookout. From Govetts Leap you can walk either north to reach Pulpit Rock or south to Evans Lookout via the falls. Although Govetts and Evans are both stunning, three other superb lookouts await your viewing pleasure and can be accessed from Blackheath. These are often missed, but are no less spectacular. The first, Pulpit Rock, can be reached by foot from Govetts (2½ km, an hour and a half) or better still by 2WD via Hat Hill Rd. The lookout, which sits on the summit of a rock pinnacle, is accessed from the car park by a short 500-m walk. From the same car park then continue north (unsealed road) to Anvil Rock, being sure not to miss the other short track to the bizarre geology of the wind eroded cave. Perry Lookdown is 1 km before Anvil Rock and a path from there descends to the valley to connect with some demanding walking trails. Also well worth a visit is Hanging Rock, a Blue Mountains icon commonly used to induce mutterings of 'ooh, well I never' on postcards and book covers. It can be reached along a rough, unsealed track (Ridgewell Rd), on the right, just beyond Blackheath heading north. Although best suited to 4WD it is just possible to take a 2WD vehicle slowly in dry conditions. But if in doubt don't. You can always resort to a local 4WD tour since most venture there. At the terminus of the track you reach the impressive Baltzer Lookout. Just to the right and out of immediate view, Hanging Rock will, on first sight, take you breath away. It is indeed aptly named and the heights are mind bending. Watch your footing and do not attempt to climb to the point, as tempting as it may be. It is a favourite abseiling spot, but only for the well equipped and insane. Like all the other lookouts on the southern fringe of the Grose Valley, sunrise is by far the best time to visit.

Megalong Valley, accessed on Megalong Valley Road west of Blackheath town centre, provides a pleasant scenic drive and is one of the most accessible and most developed of the wilderness Blue Mountains valleys. Megalong Australian Heritage Centre, **T** 4787 8688, www.megalong.cc.au, *0730-1800 daily*, is described as an 'Outback Ranch in the Mountains' and although the word 'mountains' does not (like the rest of the Blueys) exactly fit with convention, the homestead actually does, offering a whole range of activities from horse trekking (from $22) and 4WD adventures, to livestock shows. Accommodation is also available and there is a bistro restaurant.

Bells Line of Road and the Zig Zag Railway
77 km from Sydney between Windsor and Lithgow. Map 8, p255

Bells Line of Road is named after Archibald Bell, whom in 1823, at the age of 19 and with the help of the local Aboriginals, discovered the 'second' route through the Blue Mountains to Lithgow from Sydney. Starting just west of Richmond in the east, then climbing the plateau to fringe the northern rim of the Grose Valley, it provides a quieter, more sedate, scenic trip across the Great Divide and is particularly well renowned for its **gardens** which are best viewed in spring and autumn and also for its spectacular **views**.

Just beyond the village of Bilpin, west of Richmond, the huge basalt outcrop of **Mount Tomah** (1,000 m) begins to dominate the scene and supports the 28 ha cool-climate annexe of the Sydney **Botanical Gardens**, *1000-1600 daily, $6*, opened in 1987, the garden's rich volcanic soils nurture over 10,000 species, including a huge quantity of tree ferns and Rhododendrons. Although the gardens are well worth visiting in their own right, it is the views, the short walks and the restaurant that make it extra special.

Just beyond Mount Tomah is the **Walls Lookout**, with its expansive views across the Grose Valley. It requires a one-hour return walk from the Pierces Pass Track car park, but the effort it is well worth it. Back on the Bells Line of Road, and just a few kilometres further west, is the junction (north, 8 km) to the pretty village of **Mount Wilson**, famous for its English-style open gardens. These include **Linfield Park**, Mount Irvine Road, *daily, $3*, and **Nooroo**, Church Lane, *Sep- Nov, Apr-May, $3*. Also of interest is the **Cathedral of Ferns**, which is on the left, at the northern end of the village.

The **Wynnes and Du Faurs Lookouts** can also be reached from Mount Wilson and are signposted, east and west of the village centre. Back on the Bells Line of Road you can then head 8 km south at Bell to join the Great Western Highway at Mount Victoria, or continue west to Clarence (16 km) and Lithgow (29 km).

In Clarence you will find the **Zig Zag Railway, T** 6353 1795, *$14, child $11,* a masterpiece of engineering originally built between 1866 and 1869. Operated commercially up until 1910 as a supply route to Sydney, it now serves as a tourist attraction with lovingly-restored steam trains making the nostalgic 8-km (an hour and 20 minutes) journey from Clarence to Bottom Points (near CityRail's Zig Zag Station). Steam trains leave Clarence on Wednesday, Saturday and Sunday at 1100, 1300 and 1500. On other weekdays the less exciting motorized trains take over, leaving at the same time. Request drop off if you are arriving by *CityRail* from Sydney/Katoomba at the Zig Zag Station.

Jenolan Caves

T 6359 3311, www.jenolancaves.org.au   *190 km west of Sydney, 60 km south of Lithgow. There is no public transport to the Jenolan Caves, but numerous tour operators in Katoomba and Sydney can oblige with day tour packages. The main caves can only be visited by guided tour, either selectively, or in a combination package (1000-2000, 1 hour $15, child $10, 2 hours $27.50, 3-cave-combo $38.50, child $26.50.   Map, inside back cover*

Jenolan Caves, on the northern fringe of the Kanangra-Boyd National Park and south of Lithgow, comprise nine major (and 300 in total) limestone caves considered to be amongst the most spectacular in the southern hemisphere. After over 160 years of exploration and development (since their discovery in 1838 by pastoralist James Whalan), the main caves are now well geared for your viewing pleasure with a network of paths and electric lighting to guide the way and to highlight the bizarre subterranean features that have taken aeons to form. The strangely shaped stalactites (form downwards) and stalagmites (form upwards) never fail to run riot with the imagination and guided tours ensure you can learn about their formation and the cave's unique natural history. As well as guided cave tours, some other caves have been set aside for adventure caving and above ground, a network of pleasant bush trails satisfy the agoraphobics. Day tours cost about $70 increasing to $150 with a cave inspection and adventure caving. Book for activity based tours. See website or call. If you are short of time the **Lucas Cave** and **Temple of Baal Cave** caves are generally recommended and contain the widest variety of formations. **Chiefly Cave** is the most historic and, along with the **Imperial Cave,** it has partial wheelchair access. **River Cave** is said to be one of the most demanding. On your arrival at the caves you immediately encounter the **Grand Arch,** a 60 m wide, 24 m high cavern that was once used for camping and even live entertainment to the flicker of firelight. Nearby, the historic and congenial **Caves House** has been welcoming visitors since 1898.

Hawkesbury River Region

The Hawkesbury River is one of New South Wales' longest and most historic waterways and terminates in a large, scenic harbour at the northern fringe of the Ku-ring-gai National Park. The harbour itself, which is a playground for boaties, is of considerable geographical importance, containing Greater Sydney and separating it from the Central Coast. The Hawkesbury River region and the small villages of Wisemans Ferry and Street Albans in particular, provides a very pleasant day trip and quiet escape from the city.

▸▸ *See Sleeping p142, Eating and drinking p166 and Tourist information p37*

 Sights

Wisemans Ferry
Map, inside back cover

From the historic village of Wisemans Ferry, it is possible to cross the river, taking 24 hours, on the oldest ferry crossing in Australia. Remarkably it is still free. Once across head north through the beautiful **Mogo River Valley** in to the southern fringes of the **Darugh and Yengo National Parks** to **St Albans**, 21 km.

St Albans
There is no public transport to Wisemans Ferry or St Albans. By road, from the Sydney CBD, take the Pacific Highway (Hwy 1) northeast to Hornsby. Just beyond Hornsby then take a left on to Galston Rd to join the Northern Road (Hwy 36). Gradually you will leave the urban shackles behind and begin to reach scenic countryside through Glenorie and Maroota prior to sighting the magnificent Hawkesbury River at Wisemans Ferry (97 km). *Map, inside back cover*

If you feel like a walk, head a few kilometres north from the superb *Settlers Arms* (see p166) until the road takes a bend. From there you can continue on a secluded, rough track up to a natural rock lookout across the valley (ask at the pub for directions). On your return, and perhaps after another pint at the Settlers, you might want to stay in one of their charming en-suite rooms for the night or have a meal by candlelight in the cosy restaurant. Apparently, many of the old colonial pillars of society did so many years ago, in the company of young ladies looking too young to be their wives.

● *Wellums Lake Guesthouse (see p142) offers comfortable accommodation and has a great café.*

Ku-ring-gai Chase National Park

A few wealthy Sydney entrepreneurs might see Ku-ring-gai Chase as little more than 14,883 ha of wasted prime real estate, 26 km north of Sydney. Thankfully, the rugged sandstone country that fringes the mighty Hawkesbury River, with its **stunning views** *and rich array of native* **wild animals** *and plants, is safe from further suburban encroachment and has been since some bright spark (with infinite foresight) decreed it such in 1894. As well as views across Pittwater and Broken Bay (the mouth of the Hawkesbury River), from the* **West Head Lookout***, the park has some lovely bush walks, secluded beaches and regionally significant* **Aboriginal rock art***. It is also a great place to see New South Wale's much celebrated state flower in bloom – the* **warratah***. The park is named after the Guringai Aboriginals who occupied the region for over 20,000 years before the arrival of European entrepreneurs.*

⇥ See Sleeping p142, Tourist information p38 and Transport p33

◉ Sights

Without doubt the highlight of the park is the **West Head Lookout** that sits high above the peninsula overlooking **Broken Bay** and the mouth of the **Hawkesbury River**. To the north is the beginning of the central coast and **Brisbane Water National Park**, while to the west, is the tip of the northern beaches and the historic **Barrenjoey Lighthouse**. West Head is criss-crossed with walking tracks starting from West Head Road. Aboriginal rock art can be seen along the **Basin Track** (which falls to the Basin Beach campsite and the arrival/departure point of the Palm Beach ferry) and the 3.5-km **Red Hand Track** (Aboriginal Heritage Track). **Bobbin Head** at the western end of the park is a popular base for water-based activities and hosts the VIC plus several more interesting walks around the **Cowan Creek** foreshore. The VIC (see p38) can supply all the details.

Royal National Park

The 15,080-ha Royal National Park was the first national park in Australia gazetted in 1879. Before the Europeans arrived the park looked very different to the scene that confronts you today. Back then, before European farming practices and the loss of native wildlife caused drastic changes to the vegetation, the park looked something akin to English parkland with short grasslands interspersed with huge eucalyptuses. Today the vegetation has altered with smaller gums competing with much more ground cover. This ironically has created what today is the park's greatest threat – fire. More than once in the last decade the Royal has been almost completely (but temporarily) destroyed by bush fires that feed on the copious fuel that once never existed. So today, as well as providing over 100-km of walking tracks and hosting some beautiful beaches and other activities ranging from

swimming to scuba diving, the park is also a monument to humans'
destruction of the fragile Australian environment.

▸▸ *See Transport p33*

Sights

NPWS Royal National Park Visitors Centre
Farnell Ave, **T** 9542 0648. *Daily 0830-1630.*

The main hub of human activity centres around historic **Audley** at the park's northern entrance, where you will find the **NPWS Royal National Park Visitors Centre**. They can provide park maps as well as detailed information on walks and all other activities. Ranger-guided walks are often available.

Beaches

Wattamolla, **Garie** and **Burning Palms** are said to be three of the state's most beautiful beaches. The choice of walks range from the 500-m (wheelchair accessible) Bungoona Track to the 26-km Coast Track (Bundeena to Otford) that is a regional favourite. It guarantees some glorious coastal views and on occasion (from June to September) the odd whale sighting. You can hire rowboats and canoes at the Audley Boatshed, near the visitors centre, for a leisurely paddle up Kangaroo Creek. Mountain bikes are also available for hire but trail routes are limited and there is good surfing at the patrolled Garie Beach. Several freshwater pools also provide sheltered swimming with the Deer Pool (near Marley Beach) being the most popular.

Botany Bay National Park

*Botany Bay, 15-30 km south of Sydney, holds a very special place in (European) Australian history as the site of Captain Cook's first landing in April 1770. The landing site is near what is now **Kurnell** on the southern shores of Botany Bay, which along with **La Perouse** on the northern shore, comes under the auspices of the 458-ha Botany Bay National Park. As well as possessing highly significant **historical sites** for both the European and Aboriginal cultures it presents plenty of **walking opportunities** and **ocean views**. Joseph Banks, ship's naturalist on board* The Endeavour, *named the bay in 1770.*

▸▸ *See Tourist information p38 and Transport p34*

◉ Sights

Bare Island Fort

T 9247 5033. *Guided tours on Sat and Sun, $7.70, child $5.50. Map 7, G5, p254*

Within the small northern sector of the park, around **La Perouse** on the northern headland, you can take a tour of Bare Island Fort that was erected amidst wartime paranoia and the perceived threat of foreign invasion.

La Perouse Museum and Visitors Centre

T 9311 3379. *Wed-Sun 1000-1600, $5.50, child $3.30. Cable Station Anzac Pde. Map 7, G5, p254*

Also located on the northern headland is La Perouse Museum and Visitors Centre, on the actual site of the first landing of the First Fleet in 1788. The museum explores the great historical event and the fate of French explorer Captain La Perouse, as well as local Aboriginal and European heritage.

Southern sector walks

The southern sector of the park is larger and has the best walks including the short, 1-km **Monument Track**, passing several historical markers surrounding Cook's landing and the more demanding **Coast Walk** to Bailey lighthouse.

Sydney has a wealth of accommodation of all types and to suit all budgets. Most of the major luxury hotels are located around Circular Quay, Darling Harbour and the northern CBD with stunning views across the harbour or the city and with tariffs to match. More moderately priced hotels, motels and small boutique hotels are scattered around the southern city centre and inner suburbs. In the west, Glebe is a particularly good option, with interesting cafés, shops and pubs. In the east, Kings Cross is hostel-land, popular with backpackers and, separated only by a river of traffic, Darlinghurst offers a fine alternative. To the south, the well-established Bondi beachfront hotels are only yards from the famous beach. The quiet, yet central, suburb of Kirribilli across the water from The Opera House is another excellent base, with a short, cheap and spectacular ferry trip to the CBD, while further east there is no shortage of accommodation in the resort of Manly. Outside the city the Hawkesbury River Region and the Blue Mountains offer historic hotels and showpiece backpacker-hostels.

$
Price

	Sleeping codes		
LL	A$300 and over	C	A$80-109
L	A$200-299	D	A$50-79
A	A$150-199	E	A$31-49
B	A$110-149	F	A$30 and under

Prices are for a double room in high season

There are a few good bed and breakfasts in the city and these can be studied in detail through the Bed and Breakfast Council of NSW, **T** 4984 1799, www.bedandbreakfast.org.au Numerous serviced apartments are also on offer in the CBD but you are advised to book early. **Medina**, **T** 9360 1699, www.medinaaapartments.com.au are one example. Pub rooms are another option but standards vary and costs are generally quite high (from $80) For details **T** 1800 786 550, www.pubstay.com.au There are a staggering number of backpacker-hostels, with over 100 being scattered in and around the CBD, the inner suburbs and further afield in the popular beach resorts. Standards vary. Most are centred around Kings Cross. The well-established, modern YHAs are recommended. Expect to pay between $18-22 for a dorm bed, $45-55 for a double and $70 for an en-suite. Most hostels will do weekly deals for about $120 or a few dollars off the cumulative daily rate.

If you have not pre-booked any accommodation on arrival, the Sydney VIC in The Rocks is a good place to start (see p35). At any time in the peak season (October to April, when prices may rise) and especially over Christmas, the New Year and during major sporting or cultural events, pre-booking is recommended for all types of accommodation.

For detailed Northern Beaches accommodation listings get hold of the comprehensive Visitors Guide from major VICs or contact the Palm Beach and Peninsula Bed and Breakfast Group, **T** 9973 4732, www.sydneynorthernbeaches.com.au

Circular Quay and The Rocks

LL Four Seasons, 199 George St, **T** 9238 000, **F** 9251 2851, www.fourseasons.com/sydney *Map 2, D4, p248* Refurbished establishment well-placed on the edge of Circular Quay and the CBD. Offers modern, well-appointed rooms, award winning dining, specialist Australian herbal/spa therapies and also has particularly good facilities for families.

LL Observatory Hotel, 89 Kent St, **T** 9256 2222, **F** 9256 2233, www.observatoryhotel.com.au *Map 2, D6, p248* A popular, award-winning choice, in a good location between The Rocks and Darling Harbour with very classy, nicely-appointed rooms and surroundings. Fine cuisine and a distinctly cosmic pool.

LL Park Hyatt, 7 Hickson Rd, **T** 9241 1234, **F** 9256 1555, www.sydney.hyatt.com.au *Map 2, A5, p248* One of Australia's foremost hotels, not surprising given its harbourside location overlooking the Opera House and in the shadow the Harbour Bridge. Offers all the expected sophistication and mod cons. A fine ground floor restaurant offers the ideal spot to watch harbour activity. A full-scale replica of the *Bounty* is moored right outside.

LL Quay Grand, 61 Macquarie St, **T** 9256 4000, **F** 9256 4040. *Map 2, D7, p249* Located on the eastern side of Circular Quay and part of the ultramodern Opera Quays complex, providing stylish, fully self-contained apartments, with spas and stunning views across Sydney Cove and the Harbour Bridge. Definitely a place to utilize room service.

LL-L Lord Nelson Pub and Hotel, corner Kent St and Argyle St, The Rocks, **T** 9251 4044, **F** 9251 1532, hotel@lordnelson.com.au *Map 2, B2, p248* Offers very pleasant en-suite rooms above one of Sydney's best and most historic pubs. Added attractions here are home-brewed beer, food and general ambience. The pub closes fairly early at night, so noise is generally not a factor. Street parking.

L **Old Sydney Holiday Inn**, 55 George St, **T** 9252 0524, **F** 9251 2093, www.sydney.holiday-inn.com *Map 2, A5, p248* A reliable option ideally located in the heart of The Rocks, with excellent views from most rooms and especially its memorable rooftop pool and spa.

L **Russell Hotel**, 143A George St, **T** 9241 3543, **F** 9252 1652, www.therussell.com.au *Map 2, D5, p248* Small, homely, historic hotel originally built in 1882, offering a good range of elegant, period-furnished singles, en-suite standard rooms and suites. A friendly welcome and a good range of tariffs. Appealing rooftop garden and lounge bar with memorable views across the harbour.

City Centre: the CBD

LL-L **Hotel Inter-Continental**, 177 Macquarie St, **T** 9253 9000, **F** 9240 1240, www.interconti.com.au *Map 2, E7, p249* Thirty-one floor, five-star hotel located in the former 1851 Treasury Building on Macquarie Street and within a stone's throw of the Botanic Gardens and Opera House. As such it is often the first hotel of choice for visiting dignitaries. Opulent surroundings with luxury rooms and suites, an excellent café/bar and full health facilities all combine to make it one of Sydney's best.

LL-L **Wynyard Vista Hotel**, 7 York St, **T** 9290 1840, **F** 9274 1230, www.vistahotel.com.au *Map 2, F3, p248* A popular and refurbished CBD hotel offering spacious self-contained rooms and suites with excellent city views, spa and Japanese rooftop garden. Well located, with occasional attractive package deals.

L Capitol Square, Corner Campbell St and George St, **T** 9211 8633, **F** 9211 8733 www.goldspear.com.au *Map 3, E4, p250* Cosy en-suite rooms and a good restaurant – a place that can honour its claim as one of the best-placed and most affordable four-star hotels in the city centre.

L-D Y on the Park (YWCA), 5-11 Wentworth Ave, **T** 9264 2451, **T** 1800 994 994, **F** 9285 6288, www.ywca-sydney.com.au *Map 3, D6, p250* Pitched somewhere between a budget hotel and a hostel the 'Y' welcomes both male and female clients and offers a good range of clean, modern, spacious and quiet rooms with all the usual facilities. Friendly service and well placed between the city centre and social hub of Oxford Street.

A-E Alfred Park Private Hotel, 207 Cleveland St, **T** 9319 4031, hotels@g-day.aust.com *A 10-min walk south of Central Station, down Chalmers St and across Prince Alfred Park.* Former home of a whaling captain with 14 children it now serves as a cross between a budget hotel and a backpacker-hostel, offering the peace and quiet lacking in the better-known city establishments. It is well kept and very clean, offering tidy dorms, and spacious singles, doubles and twins. There is also a pleasant courtyard, modern facilities and free guest parking.

A-E Hotel Bakpak(s), 412 Pitt St, **T** 9211 4588, Freecall **T** 1800 013 186 (the newest) and 417 Pitt St, **T** 9211 5115, Freecall **T** 1800 813 522, www.bakpakgroup.com *Map 3, E4, p250* A pair of backpackers, both popular (mainly due to their position) offering a good range of clean, modern rooms most with en-suite, TV, fridge and telephone. The services, which include tour bookings, and onward travel, are also above average.

A-E Millett's OZ, Level 1, 161 Castlereagh St, **T** 9283 6599, www.wakeup.com.au *Map3, A5, p250* A newly refurbished budget option in the heart of the city with nicely-appointed doubles/twins, some en-suite, and a range of dorms. It also has a café, bar, travel desk and employment information.

B George Street Private Hotel, 700A George St, **T/F** 9211 1800. *Map 3, E4, p250* Affordable hotel, well-situated right next door to the Capitol Theatre and all the action on George Street, in Chinatown and Haymarket.

B-D Wanderers Backpackers, 477 Kent St, **T** 1800 424 444, **T** 9267 7718, www.wanderersonkent.com.au *Map3, B3, p250* A modern, purpose-built facility with large fine doubles, twins and dorms. There are no kitchen facilities but there is a cheap café and bar on the ground floor and a rash of eateries nearby. Also has to be the only backpackers with a stand-up solarium.

C-D Sydney Central YHA, Corner Pitt St and Rawson Pl, **T** 9281 9111, sydcentral@yhansw.org.au *Map 3, A5, p250* Hugely popular and ideally placed next to Central Station and the main interstate bus depot. The huge heritage building, has over 500 beds split in to a vast range of dorms, doubles and twins, with some en-suite. It also offers all mod cons including pool, sauna, café, bar, internet, mini-mart, TV rooms and employment and travel desks. Its only downfall may however be its size – for some it will be too impersonal.

Darling Harbour and Chinatown

LL Carlton Crest Hotel, 169 Thomas St, **T/F** 9281 6888, www.carltonhotels.com.au/sydney *Map3, G2, p250* Noted for its interesting architecture and popular pre-theatre restaurant. Also offers fine views back across the city centre, especially from its rooftop garden/outdoor pool.

LL-L Novotel, 100 Murray St, **T** 9301 2756, **F** 9301 2756, www.novotel.com.au *Map 3, B1, p250* Reliable, large chain hotel and something of a landmark ideally located over looking Darling Harbour with all its major tourist attractions. Standard rooms and suites with great views (especially at night), good French restaurant (**Baudin's**), friendly service and well equipped for family groups. Easy downtown access on the Light/Mono Rail.

LL-L Star City Hotel and Apartments, 80 Pyrmont St, Pyrmont, **T** 9657 8393, **F** 9475 0180, www.starcity.com.au A fine choice amongst the many modern luxury hotels fringing Darling Harbour with the added appeal of the casino, theatres, nightclubs, pubs, restaurants and shopping all on-site. Well-appointed standard rooms and suites with harbour views. Good mid-week or weekend specials.

LL-A Aarons Hotel, 37 Ultimo Rd, **T** 9281 5555, **F** 9281 2666. *Map 3, F3, p250* No nonsense, value option set right in the heart of the Chinatown buzz with basic en-suite rooms, suites and deluxe rooms. Lively café with breakfast included.

L-A Glasgow Arms Hotel, 527 Harris St, Ultimo, **T** 9211 2354. *Map3, E1, p250* Good value, friendly hotel/pub-stay option located on the edge of Darling Harbour. Basic yet cosy rooms, entertaining bar (last orders by about 2230). Affordable pub restaurant with a courtyard downstairs.

City West: Glebe to Parramatta

LL-L Trickett's Luxury B&B, 270 Glebe Point Rd, **T** 9552 1141, **F** 9692 9462. *Map 4, C1, p252* Beautifully restored Victorian mansion, decorated with antiques and Persian rugs, offering seven spacious, nicely furnished en-suite rooms. Well worth the trip from the city centre.

L-A Rooftop Motel, 146-148 Glebe Point Rd, **T** 9660 7777.
Map 4, F3, p252 No-nonsense, quiet and clean motel, ideally
located to all amenities. Single, doubles, twins and family rooms,
pool and breakfast if required.

L-D Alishan International Guesthouse, 100 Glebe Point Rd,
T 9566 4048, www.alishan.com.au *Map 4, G4, p252* Pitched
halfway between a small hotel and a quality hostel. Spacious,
renovated Victorian mansion with spotless doubles, twins and
family en-suite rooms, all with TV and fridge. Shared
accommodation also available and the facilities are generally
excellent. A great value budget option, especially for couples
looking for a quiet place away from the city centre.

A-E Billabong Gardens, 5-11 Egan St, Newtown, **T** 9550 3236,
Free call **T** 1800 806 419, www.billabonggardens.com.au One of
very few accommodation options in Newtown offering a good range
of en-suite rooms, standard rooms and dorms with a fully equipped
kitchen, lounge with TV, Internet and a heated pool. A good choice
as an alternative to the mainstream establishments and locations.

B-D Wattle House, 44 Hereford St, **T** 9552 4997,
www.wattlehouse.com.au *Map 4, F1, p252* A lovingly restored
Victorian house, smaller than the competition with a cosy, homely
feel and welcoming, caring owners. It has great double rooms and
is especially popular among those looking for a quieter more
intimate place to stay. Book well in advance.

B-E Glebe Village Backpackers, 256 Glebe Point Rd, **T** 9660
8133, Freecall **T** 1800 801 983, glebevillage@bakpak.com.au *Map
4, C1, p252* Located next door to the Glebe Point YHA, the Village
is a large, working backpacker's favourite. It offers a range of dorms
and a few basic doubles and is friendly, laid back and of course

★ **Rooms with a view**

Best

- Park Hyatt (Circular Quay), p122
- Quay Grand (Circular Quay), p122
- Novotel (Darling Harbour), p126
- Swiss Grand (Bondi), p133
- Jonah's (Palm Beach), p139

prides itself in finding work for guests. In-house café, pick-ups and regular day tours to beaches and other locations.

D-E Glebe Point YHA, 262 Glebe Point Rd, **T** 9692 8418, glebe@yhansw.org.au *Map 4, C1, p252* A popular place with a nice atmosphere, offering fairly small twin and four-share dorms and modern facilities throughout. Barbecues on the roof are a speciality. Regular shuttle into the city and bus stops nearby.

City East: Kings Cross to Bondi

Kings Cross, Potts Point and Wooloomooloo

LL W Hotel, 6 Cowper Wharf Rd, Woolloomooloo, **T** 9331 9000, **F** 9331 9031, www.Whotels.com *Map 2, H10, p249* Stylish, warehouse-style, luxury hotel opened in 2000 and the showpiece of the Woolloomooloo Wharf. Has the added attraction of fine restaurants and a fine flotilla of luxury launches right outside. Sumptuous, contemporary rooms often used by visiting pop stars and well-heeled CEOs. Practically on the doorstep is an older Sydney institution – **Harry's Café de Wheels** (see p157) – where you can be assured of the best and the cheapest pies in the city.

LL-A Victoria Court, 122 Victoria St, Potts Point, **T** 9357 3200, Freecall **T** 1800 630 505, **F** 9357 7606, www.VictoriaCourt.com.au *Map 3, A11, p251* A delightful and historic boutique hotel in a quiet location, complete with antiques, well-appointed en-suite rooms, fireplaces and four-poster beds. The courtyard conservatory is a highlight.

L The Barclay, 17 Bayswater Rd, Kings Cross, **T/F** 9358 6133 barclayhotel@bigpond.com *Map 3, C12, p251* Newly renovated, classy and quiet, but still set right in the heart of all action. Rated three-star with all the relevant modern facilities. A nice atmosphere.

L-A Macleay Serviced Apartments, 28 Macleay St, Potts Point, **T** 9357 7755, macleay@nectar.com.au *Map 3, A12, p251* Friendly and reliable apartment option at the edge of Potts Point with a great view across the harbour. Short walk in to Kings Cross or the restaurants at Woolloomooloo Wharf.

B-E Backpackers Headquarters, 79 Bayswater Rd, Kings Cross, **T** 9331 6180. *Map 3, C12, p251* Immaculately kept and well run, the layout is a little odd but otherwise a fine choice in a quiet location, yet still close to all the action.

C-D Blue Parrot, 87 Mcleay St, Potts Point, **T** 9356 4888, Freecall **T** 1800 252 299. *Map 3, A12, p251* Towards Potts Point (therefore quieter) and a new player on the scene. As such, it has all new fixtures and fittings, which is an attraction in itself. Open fire.

C-D Kanga House 141 Victoria St, Kings Cross, **T** 9357 7879. *Map 3, B11, p251* Relaxed hostel offering a warm welcome. If you are lucky you may be able to secure a room with a view of the Opera House, something that would add a zero to your tariff in the city.

Sleeping

Cross hostels

There are over 35 backpacker hostels in and around Kings Cross. With such fierce competition you will find standards are generally good. All the hostels try to lure guests with some gimmick or other, be it a 'good time' reputation, its age, a café, free meal tickets, air-con in the rooms as opposed to a fan, one night in seven free (mainly winter) and even beer. All offer attractive weekly rates and most have internet, offer free pick-ups and assistance with onward travel and job search. If you intend to stay in Kings Cross for some time the best thing to do is to pre-book a couple of nights in one then, if you are dissatisfied, shop around until you find one that suits your particular taste. Most of the hostels are located along Victoria St, Orwell St or on the main drag, (and in the heart of the action) Darlinghurst Rd.

C-E Eva's, 6-8 Orwell St, Potts Point, **T** 9358 2185, www.evasbackpackers.com.au or www.nomadsworld.com *Map 3, A12, p251* Clean, well-managed hostel that offers a distinctly homely feel. Arty rooms, some en-suite. Rooftop space used for social barbecues and offering great views across the city.

C-E Funk House, 23 Darlinghurst Rd, Kings Cross, **T** 9358 6455, Freecall **T** 1800 247 600 goodtimes@funkhouse.com.au *Map 3, B12, p251* Set right on Darlinghurst Road, one for the younger party set. Zany artwork dons the walls and doors. Three- to four-bed dorms and double/twins all with fridge, TV and fan. Lots of freebies. Their almost legendary rooftop barbecues are a great place to meet others. Good job search assistance.

C-E Jolly Swagman, 27 Orwell St, **T** 9358 6400, Kings Cross, Freecall **T** 1800 805 870, www.jollyswagman.com.au *Map 3, B12,* *p251* A buzzing hostel in the heart of the action. Professionally run with facilities including TV, fridge and fan in most rooms. Excellent travel desk and job search assistance. Sociable atmosphere. 24-hour check in, fast internet and free beer on arrival.

C-E Original Backpackers Lodge, 160-162 Victoria St, Kings Cross, **T** 9356 3232, www.originalbackpackers.com.au *Map 3, B11, p251* Possibly the best hostel in Kings Cross and certainly one of the best equipped and managed. The historic house is large and homely, comfortably furnished, offering a great range of double, twin, TV, fridge and fans (heated in winter). There is a great open courtyard in which to socialize or enjoy a barbecue. Cable TV. The staff are always on hand to help with onward travel, job seeking or things to see and do while Blinkey the boxer dog can ease any loneliness for the homesick dog owner. Book ahead.

C-E The Palms (Nomads), 23 Hughes St, Kings Cross, **T** 9357 1199, Freecall **T** 1800 737 773. *Map 3, A12, p251* Fine, friendly place with a relaxed atmosphere and a very social courtyard out front. All the usual facilities with rooms including TV and fridge.

C-E The Pink House, 6-8 Barncleuth Square, Kings Cross, **T/F** 9358 1689, Freecall **T** 1800 806 384, thepinkh@qd.com.au *Map 3, B12, p251* A historic mansion offering a homely feel that is lacking in many of the other Kings Cross hostels. Deservingly popular, especially for those tired of the party scene. Lots of quiet corners and a shady courtyard in which to find peace of mind. Large dorms and some good doubles. Cable TV and free internet.

C-E Rucksack Rest, 9 McDonald St, Potts Point, **T/F** 9358 2348. *Map 2, G12, p248* Long-established private hostel, basic and a little tired looking, but good value, in a quiet location and with good double rooms. Good general travel and city advice.

C-E **Travellers Rest**, 156 Victoria St, Kings Cross, **T** 9358 4606.
Map 3, B11, p251 Well-established hostel especially popular with
long-stayers. Dorm, single, twin and doubles some with TV, fridge,
fan, phone and kettle. Attractive weekly rates.

C-E **Virgin Backpackers**, 144 Victoria St, Kings Cross, **T** 9357
4733, Freecall **T** 1800 667 255, www.vbackpackers.com.au *Map 3,
B11, p251* Quite modern and chic the 'V' offers good facilities: a
nice balance between the lively and quiet. Tidy doubles and twins
with TV and fridge and dorms. Well-travelled, helpful managers,
and an internet café with good cheap meals.

Darlinghurst, Paddington and Surry Hills

LL **Hotel Altamont**, 207 Darlinghurst Rd, Darlinghurst, **T** 9360
6000, **F** 9369 7096, www.altamont.com.au *Map 3, D11, p251* No
less classy than L'Otel opposite, yet supporting a more traditional
decor with beautiful spacious deluxe rooms with wooden floors
and fittings. Very comfortable, relaxed and friendly all of which
combines with the ambience and decor to offer great value.

LL **Kirketon**, 229 Darlinghurst Rd, Darlinghurst, **T** 9332 2011,
F 9332 2011, www.kirketon.com.au *Map 3, D11, p251* The decor
here is modern, chic and minimalist with a bar and restaurant to
match. In summary it is all very 'contemporary Sydney' with all
sorts of interesting retro touches in interior design. Gym, good
restaurant and valet parking.

LL **L'Otel**, 114 Darlinghurst Rd, Darlinghurst, **T** 9360 6868,
F 9331 4536, www.lotel.com.au *Map 3, D11, p251* Very classy,
chic establishment, yet given its hip minimalist decor perhaps not
everyone's cup of tea. Even the carpet supports the hotel's name
so there is no forgetting where you are no matter how good the
night out. Personable service and a fine restaurant attached.

LL Medina on Crown, 359 Crown St, Surry Hills, **T** 9360 6666, **F** 9361 5965, www.medinaapartments.com.au *Map 3, H8, p251* Particularly well-equipped mid-range option in a quiet location, offering spacious, well-appointed one- or two-bedroom serviced apartments. Café, gym, heated pool and off street parking.

A Royal Sovereign Hotel, corner Liverpool St and Darlinghurst Rd, Darlinghurst, **T** 9331 3672, www.darlobar.com.au *Map 3, E10, p251* Offers a range of spotless, newly-refurbished rooms above the popular 'Darlo' bar. Shared bathroom facilities. Great value for money and still within walking distance of Kings Cross. Last orders at the bar before 2300 and the noise from downstairs is not said to be a problem.

C-E Kangaroo Bakpak, 665 South Dowling St, Surry Hills, **T** 9319 5915, www.kangaroobakpak.com.au *Off the southwest corner of Moore Park.* Relaxed, friendly backpacker option close to Centennial Park with colourful, well-appointed rooms and a leafy garden. Offers a pleasant alternative to the more manic budget options in Kings Cross. Located right beside a busy main road, but traffic noise is minimal.

Bondi

LL-L Ravesi's, corner Campbell Pde and Hall St, Bondi, **T** 9365 4422, **F** 9365 1481, www.ravesis.com.au *Map 6, G3, p253* Slightly less obvious and intimate than the *Swiss Grand*, Ravesi's offers good value three-star standard rooms, standard suites and luxury split level suites, most with balconies overlooking all the action. The refurbished balcony restaurant is also one of the best in the area.

LL Swiss Grand, corner Campbell Pde and Beach Rd, Bondi, **T** 9365 5666, Freecall **T** 1800 655 252, **F** 9365 5330, www.swissgrand.com.au *Map 6, F4, p253* The largest and most spectacular of the beachfront hotel options. Luxury suites with all mod cons, excellent views, two restaurants, gaming bar and a particularly interesting foyer. The rooftop pool is stunning and a great escape from the hordes on the beach. Occasionally offers good value 'Getaway' deals that are mainly directed at couples. Undercover parking and airport transfers.

L-A **Bondi Beachside Inn**, 152 Campbell Pde, Bondi, **T** 9130 5311, **F** 9365 2646, www.bondiinn.com.au *Map 6, G3, p253*   A beachfront option, pitched somewhere between a hotel and motel, offering tidy rooms and suites with kitchenettes and ocean views that match the more expensive hotels. A glut of restaurants just outside the door is an added attraction, as is the proximity of the beach.

L-A **Hotel Bondi**, 178 Campbell Pde, Bondi, **T** 9130 3271, **F** 9130 7974, www.hotelbondi.com.au *Map 6, G3, p253*   A more traditional hotel with a popular public bar downstairs, a good café and a nightclub/performance space, *Zinc*, where you can shake your pants to live bands and DJs, or put your potting skills to the test in a pool competition.

A **City Beach Motor Inn**, 99 Curlewis St, Bondi, **T** 9365 3100, **F** 9365 0231. *Map 6, F2, p253*   Good for families or couples or if you are looking for a quiet motel within walking distance of the beach. Choice of refurbished executive suites or older standard units, some with spa. Breakfast on request. Secure parking.

B-E **Noah's Bondi Beach Backpackers**, 2 Campbell Pde, Bondi, **T** 9365 7100, www.noahs.com.au *Map 6, 3H, p253*   A large establishment perched on the hill overlooking the beach. Popular due to its position and price, but certainly not the quietest. Former hotel rooms have been converted to better than average dorms, twins and doubles (some with ocean views). A rooftop barbecue area also offers great views.

C-D Indy's Bondi Beach Backpackers, 35A Hall St, Bondi, **T** 9365 4900, www.indys.com.au *Map 6, G2, p253* One of the most popular budget options in Bondi. Modern, friendly with all the usual facilities, including doubles and twins with TV, fridge and fans and a very comfortable cable TV room where you can catch that vital footy game back home. It has a lively sociable atmosphere and the sheer range of free hires, from surfboards to roller blades, provide an added attraction.

C-E Lamrock Lodge Backpackers, 19 Lamrock Ave, Bondi, **T** 9130 5063, www.lamrocklodge.com.au *Map 6, G2, p253* New, modern facilities and all rooms, dorm, single, twin and double, have cable TV, fridge, kitchenette and microwave. Management have their finger on the pulse with regard to travellers' needs. Good value.

Coogee

LL Crowne Plaza Hotel, 242 Arden St, **T** 9315 7600, **F** 9315 9100, www.crowneplaza.com Coogee's largest chain hotel, fully refurbished, offering nicely furnished rooms or suites with standard facilities and great views across the ocean. Popular restaurant, a bar and secure under-cover parking.

LL-A Coogee Bay Boutique Hotel, 9 Vicar St, **T** 9665 0000, **F** 9664 2103, www.coogeebayhotel.com.au Very pleasant, refurbished, boutique-style rooms in addition to good traditional pub-style options. Both types are well appointed, en-suite, have ocean views and are good value. The hotel itself is a social focus in Coogee both day and night.

B-D Coogee Beachside Hotel, 171 Arden St, **T** 9665 1162. Quiet, personable budget option where lone travellers, especially girls, are well looked after. Adequate rooms and standard facilities with free breakfast.

B-E Coogee Beachside Backpackers, 178/172 Coogee Bay Rd, **T** 9315 8511, www.sydneybeachside.com.au Essentially two suburban houses full of character (Wizard of Oz and Beachside) that combine under the Coogee Beachside banner. The rooms, especially the doubles, are excellent. Good facilities, friendly staff with good work contacts. Five minutes' walk to the beach. Ask about flat shares if you intend to stay long term.

C-E Surfside Backpackers, 186 Arden St, **T** 9315 7888, www.surfsidebackpackers.com.au Largest of Coogee's three backpackers and the closest to the beach. It is a very sociable place with a solid reputation and all the usual facilities.

City North: Manly to the Northern Beaches

Manly

LL Corunna Manor, 2 Osborne Rd, **T** 04 0741 1510, corunna@tradepac.com.au *Off East Esplanade.* Luxury B&B option set in a century-old homestead. Spacious rooms with veranda (one with spa bath). Internet and library. Short walk from the ferry terminal and Manly Beach.

LL Manly Pacific Park Royal, 55 North Steyne, **T** 9977 7666, **F** 9977 7822, www.parkroyal.com.au *Map 5, B4, p253* The most luxurious of Manly's numerous hotels overlooking the main beach and providing spacious rooms and suites with private balcony, a rooftop pool, spa, sauna, gym and a good restaurant. Under-cover parking is also provided.

LL Manly Paradise Motel and Apartments, 54 North Steyne, **T** 9977 5799, www.manlyparadise.com.au *Map 5, B4, p253* One of the best apartment options in Manly. Beachfront with ocean views, private balconies and rooftop pool.

LL-L Periwinkle Guest House, corner East Esplanade and Ashburner St, **T** 9977 4668, www.periwinkle.citysearch.com.au An 1895 historic homestead that gets consistently good reviews. Centrally located, yet quiet and full of character. There is a choice of 18 singles, doubles or triples with shared bathrooms or en-suite rooms. Kitchen barbecue and laundry. Complimentary breakfast, good weekly rates and local work contacts.

L Manly Lodge Boutique Hotel, 22 Victoria Pde, **T** 9977 8655, **F** 9976 2090, www.manlylodge.com.au *Map 5, E4, p253* A more homely option than the chain hotels or apartments located in one of the quieter streets near Manly beach. Nicely appointed en-suite doubles, twins, family rooms and suites, some with spa. Complimentary breakfast.

L-D Manly Beach Hut, 7 Pine St (corner of Whistler and Pine Sts), **T** 9977 8777, **F** 9977 8766, www.manlybeachhut.com.au *Map 5, A3, p253* Although also serving as a backpackers, the Beach Hut offers some quality, spotless and good-value twins and doubles for couples, or the more mature independent traveller, as well as shared accommodation. Pleasant courtyard area and only a short stroll to the beach.

L-D Steyne Hotel, corner Ocean Beach and The Corso, **T** 9977 4977, **F** 9977 5645, stay@steynehotel.com.au *Map 5, C4, p253* An older, cheaper and traditional pub-style hotel set right on the busy

Sydney motor parks and campsites

C-E **Lane Cove River Caravan Park**, Plassey Rd, North Ryde, (14 km northwest of the CBD) **T** 9888 9133, lccp@npws.nsw.gov.au Although nothing spectacular it offers powered and non-powered sites and a few basic yet comfortable cabins in a bush setting within the bounds of the Lane Cove National Park. The site is owned and operated by the National Parks and Wildlife Service.

A-D **Sydney Lakeside Narrabeen**, Lake Park Rd, Narrabeen (26 km north of the CBD), **T** 9913 7845, www.sydneylakeside.com.au Good range of quality villas and bungalows as well as powered and non-powered sites all close to the beach and the lagoon. Kitchen and barbecues.

A-D **Grand Pines Tourist Park**, 112 Alfred St, Ramsgate, (17 km south of the CBD), **T** 9529 7329, www.thegrandpines.com.au Close to the airport, and on public transport routes, offering deluxe en-suite, standard cabins and powered sites, but no tents are allowed.

Corso and opposite the beach, with standard, deluxe and backpacker rooms (some en-suite with ocean views) and competitive rates that include breakfast. Bottle shop (liquor store), bar, bistro and beer garden downstairs.

L-E Manly Beach Resort, 6 Carlton St, **T** 9977 4188, **F** 9977 0524, www.manlyview.com.au *Map 5, A3, p253* Good three-star motel option. Single, double, and twin rooms (some en-suite) and breakfast is included. Tidy backpacker-style accommodation also available. Pool and spa.

B-D Manly Backpackers Beachside, 28 Raglan St, **T** 9977 3411, manlybackpack@bigpond.com.au *Map 5, B3, p253* Well-rated, well-placed and well-run, with some en-suite doubles and small dorms. Good kitchen, plenty of assistance organizing the best local activities and free boogie boards. No in-house internet but there is an internet café nearby.

Kirribilli

B-D Glenferrie Lodge, 12A Carabella St, **T** 9955 1685, www.glenferrielodge.com.au A vast, 68-room Victorian mansion that is under new management and looks set to make its mark on the quality budget accommodation scene. The range of shared, single, twin or doubles is superb with some having their own balconies (from which, apparently, you might see Australia's Prime Minister John Howard jogging past from his Sydney Residence nearby). Cheap dinners are on offer nightly. Very friendly.

C-E Wharf Backpackers, 48 East Esplanade, **T** 9977 2800. *Opposite the ferry terminal.* Popular, cheap backpacker option located right opposite the ferry terminal. Arty interior with colourful doubles, twins and a variety of dorms. Nice relaxing garden out back. Cable TV.

Northern beaches

LL Jonah's, 69 Bynya Rd, Palm Beach, **T** 9974 5599, **F** 9974 1212, www.jonahs.com.au *Map 7, A6, p254* A luxury boutique hotel and restaurant set high on the hill over looking Whale Beach. Offers seven very cosy rooms with spectacular views. Excellent place to escape the city. The restaurant is French Mediterranean.

B-E Collaroy YHA (Sydney Beachhouse), 4 Collaroy St, Collaroy Beach, **T** 9981 1177, www.sydneybeachhouse.com.au *Catch the L90* *or L88 bus from Central, Wynyard or QVB. Map 7, C6, p254* One of Sydney's best backpackers offering tidy dorms, twins, doubles and family rooms (some en-suite) and great facilities, including a heated pool, spacious kitchen, dining areas, TV rooms, free equipment hire, organized day trips and even free didgeridoo lessons. It deserves its reputation as one of the best backpackers in the city. Book ahead.

Blue Mountains

LL-L Carrington Hotel, 15-47 Katoomba St, Katoomba, **T** 47821111, **F** 4782 7033, www.thecarrington.com.au *Map 8, E3, p255* An old classic built originally in 1882 and lavishly refurbished in 1998. It offers an elegant, historic and congenial atmosphere, with everything from open fires and stained-glass windows, to a classy billiards room. The rooms are beautifully appointed and there is a fine restaurant, a bar, nightclub and a spa.

LL-L Jemby-Rinjah Eco Lodge, 336 Evans Lookout Rd, Blackheath, **T** 47877622, www.jembyrinjahlodge.com.au *Map 8, D2, p255* One- or two- bedroom, self-contained, modern cabins (one with a Japanese hot tub), log fires, all in a beautiful bush setting close to the lookout and walks. Dinner, bed and breakfast packages are also available.

LL Hydro Majestic Hotel, Great Western Highway, Medlow Bath, **T** 47881002, **F** 4788 1063, www.hydromajestic.com.au *Map 8, E2, p255* Worth staying in purely for the historical aspects, the art-deco architecture and especially the views. Completely renovated inside, it offers luxury rooms and suites (some with spa and valley views) plus all the amenities you might expect.

LL-L Peppers Fairmont Resort, 1 Sublime Point Rd, Leura, **T** 47825222, F 9999 4332 www.peppers.com.au *Map 8, E3, p255*

Peppers is perhaps the most high-profile resort accommodation in the region and has a fine reputation, offering luxuriously appointed rooms and suites, as well as all the usual amenities including a restaurant, bar, pool, spa and massage. It is also very handy for the golf course.

L-B Glenella Guesthouse, 56 Govett's Leap Rd, Blackheath, **T** 47878352, **F** 4787 6114. *Map 8, D2, p255* A well-known, surprisingly affordable, historic guesthouse built in 1905, with a reputable restaurant plus comforts including sauna, open fires and cable TV.

LL-C Imperial Hotel, 1 Station St, Mount Victoria, **T** 47871878, www.bluemts.com.au/hotelimperial *Map 8, C2, p255* Reputedly the oldest tourist hotel in Australia. Beautifully restored, it still retains and offers a wide range of well-appointed rooms from the traditional to the four-poster with double spa. Breakfast included, good restaurant, bar and live entertainment at the weekends.

LL-F Jenolan Caves Resort, **T** 63593322, www.jenolancaves.com.au Includes the gracious Caves House that offers a range of traditional rooms and suites, as well as modern lodge units, self-contained cottages and a basic campsite. The resort is very well equipped with an à la carte restaurant, bistro, bar and a host of organized activities.

A-E Katoomba Blue Mountains YHA, 207 Katoomba St, Katoomba, **T** 47821416, bluemountains@yhansw.org.au *Map 8, E3, p255* Pitched both at mid-range and backpackers markets, this beautifully renovated hostel, within an art-deco building, is something of a showpiece for the YHA and is fast developing a reputation as one of its best. Modern, spacious, well equipped, friendly and most certainly recommended. Trips are gladly arranged and there is bike hire and internet.

A-E Katoomba Falls Caravan Park, Katoomba Falls Rd, Katoomba, **T** 47821835. *Map 8, E3, p255* Well-located in the heart of the action with standard cabins, powered and non-powered sites and a camp kitchen.

C/E Blue Mountains Backpackers, 190 Bathurst St, Katoomba, **T** 1800624226. *Map 8, E3, p255* Established and sociable hostel with standard facilities. The owner also runs the Katoomba Adventure Centre, so there is plenty of good advice on hand concerning local activities, especially walks.

Hawkesbury River Region

L-A Settlers Arms, 1 Wharf St, St Albans, **T** 4568 2111. Superb 1830s historic pub with its tiny stone-floored bar, charming en-suite rooms and outdoor seating area. It is an ideal spot for a lazy afternoon or a quiet, romantic overnight stay. Small cosy restaurant on-site.

A Wellum's Lake Guesthouse, Lot 1 Wellum's Lake, Settlers Rd (3 km south of St Albans), **T** 4568 2027, **F** 4568 2027, cbr@ix.net.au Another fine alternative located near St Albans, offering comfortable cabins or cottage-style accommodation and a great café on site overlooking Wellum's Lake.

Ku-ring-gai Chase National Park

C-E YHA Pittwater, via Halls Wharf, Morning Bay, via Church Pt, **T** 9999 2196, pittwater@rivernet.com.au *Map 7, B5, p254* A real getaway, located in the park and accessible only by ferry. Offers dorms and a few doubles, plenty of walking and water-based activities or simple peace and quiet. Take supplies and book ahead.

Sydney is replete with over 3,000 restaurants, brigades of world-class chefs, a rich array of fresh local produce (including kangaroo, snapper, barramundi, emu or crocodile). As well as excellent food there are also gallons of great national wines with which to wash it all down. As a general rule you will find the most lauded of the fine dining establishments that specialize in Modern Australian cuisine in and around Circular Quay, The Rocks, the CBD and Darling Harbour, however pockets of international speciality abound, from chow mien in Chinatown to pasta in Paddington. Sydney's thriving café culture is centred around the suburbs of Darlinghurst, Glebe, Newtown and the eastern beaches of Bondi and Bronte, which are also perfect locations for a congenial Sunday brunch. Choose from seafood and views from Doyle's on the beach in Watson's Bay, a cruise of the menus one evening along Newton's King Street (full of character), a night out overlooking Darling Harbour (very moderne) or a leisurely breakfast at Bondi or Bronte (so Sydney).

The cheapest eateries in **Circular Quays** are to be found around the ferry terminals but unless you are desperate or want to put your cholesterol levels off the scale, these are best avoided.

Vegetarians should perhaps avoid **Chinatown** restaurants since they are not shy about displaying various sea creatures in squalid tanks prior to being boiled alive for your gastronomic pleasure.

Glebe is home to many laid-back cafés and good pubs and in many ways the same applies to **Newtown**, except that Kings Street also has no end of attractive little restaurants offering everything from curry to charred emu. If you have time a night cruising the menus of Kings Street is an experience in itself.

Kings Cross and **Woolloomooloo** offer eclectic choices, from the fast food outlets of Kings Cross, to the chic and expensive options to be found along The Wharf at Woolloomooloo.

Although receiving less attention than the eccentricities of Glebe and Newtown, **Leichhardt** is well known for its Italian connections and subsequently its eateries and cafés. There are numerous places to enjoy a fine espresso, gelato or the full lasagne, with Norton Street the main focus (see box, p157).

Darlinghurst and **Paddington** combine to dominate the city's café scene; Oxford Street, Victoria Street and Darlinghurst Road in particular. But it is not all baguettes and baristas, with some of the best restaurants in town to be found scattered amongst them.

A leisurely weekend breakfast at **Bronte**, followed by the clifftop walk to Bondi, is highly recommended. As you might expect, many of **Manly**'s eating choices come on the end of a cone, between two sorry bits of white bread, or in dripping sheets of grease proof paper. There are no end of cheap takeaways along the concourse between the ferry wharf and Manly Beach, but shop around and you will find more healthy and unusual alternatives.

Being so close to Sydney and attracting so many rampant gourmands, **Katoomba** and the **Blue Mountains** generally pride themselves in offering some classy restaurants and fine cuisine.

Circular Quay and The Rocks

$$$$ Bel Mondo, Level 3, Argyle Stores, 18 Argyle St, **T** 9241 3700. *Tue-Fri lunch, daily dinner. Map 2, C4, p248* Set in a former elevated warehouse, which provides excellent views and plenty of atmosphere, Bel Mondo offers fine Italian cuisine and a good wine list. Service is excellent and reviews consistently good.

$$$$ Guillaume at Bennelong Restaurant, Opera House Concourse, **T** 9250 7578. *Mon-Sat dinner , Fri lunch. Map 2, B7, p249* Housed within one of the smaller 'shells' of the Opera House complex the renovated Bennelong offers unusual aesthetics and great food. Recent reports suggest this 'icon within the icon' under the meat cleaver of chef Guillaume Brahimi will more than live up to its former excellent reputation.

$$$$ Quay, Upper Level, Overseas Passenger Terminal, Circular Quay West, **T** 9251 5600. *Mon-Fri lunch, daily dinner. Map 2, B5, p248* Closer to the water and offering unobstructed views of the bridge and the Opera House, the European-influenced Quay Restaurant is very expensive, but a memorable experience with excellent seafood.

$$$$ **The Rockpool**, 107 George St, **T** 92521 8888. *Mon-Fri lunch, Mon-Sat dinner*. *Map 2, C4, p248* Located in the heart of The Rocks the Rockpool is a firm favourite, offering highly imaginative cuisine with a European/Asian edge. Seafood is recommended and there is a good wine list.

$$$ **Aqua Luna**, 2/18, Opera Quays, East Circular Quay, **T** 9251 3177. *Mon-Fri lunch, daily dinner*. *Map 2, C7, p249* Housed within the 'Toaster' Aqua Luna is a slick-looking establishment, known for its fine and imaginative Italian and Modern Australian cuisine, its views and a lively, distinctly trendy atmosphere.

$$$ **Café Sydney**, Level 5, 31 Alfred St, **T** 9251 8683. *Daily lunch, Mon-Sat dinner*. *Map 2, E6, p248* Set high above Circular Quay at the top of Customs House, Café Sydney is a favourite with city workers, offering superb views and al fresco dining. The food is traditional Modern Australian and there is a good atmosphere with occasional live jazz.

$$$ **Wharf Restaurant**, Pier 4, Hickson Rd, Walsh Bay **T** 9250 1761. *Mon-Sat lunch and dinner*. *Map 2, A3, p248* Off the beaten track and a firm local favourite located at the end of one of the historic Walsh Bay pier beside the Sydney Theatre Company, offering a great atmosphere and wonderful views of the busy harbour. Ideal for a classy, pre-performance dinner. Modern Australian cuisine.

$$ **Australian Hotel**, 100 Cumberland St, **T** 9247 2229. *Daily, lunch and dinner*. *Map 2, C4, p248* A fine venue for a true taste of Aussie food and beer, with a relaxed atmosphere. Generally good value, with al fresco dining and a menu which includes pizza, croc, emu and roo steaks.

Eating and drinking

$$ MCA Café, 140 George St, **T** 9241 4253. *Mon-Fri lunch, Sat and Sun breakfast and lunch. Map 2, C5, p248* Located in the Museum of Contemporary Art, the MCA is ideally placed next to all the action on Circular Quay. It is a bit expensive but worth it and the seafood is excellent.

City Centre: the CBD

$$$$ Forty One, Level 41, Chiefly Tower, Chiefly Sq, **T** 9221 2500. *Mon-Fri lunch, Mon-Sat dinner. Map 2, F6, p248* Popular, classy, spacious and congenial restaurant with excellent city views. With such a location one might expect the food to be insignificant, but it will not disappoint. Modern Australian. Book well in advance.

$$$$ Restaurant VII, 7 Bridge St, **T** 9252 7777. *Tue-Fri 1200-1400, 1900-2200, Sat 1900-2200. Map 2, E5, p248* One of the newest up-market restaurants in Sydney, earning a good reputation and offering imaginative Japanese cuisine with a French influence. Excellent attention to detail and great cuisine, but someone (you) has to pay for it!

$$$$ Tetsuya's, 729 Kent St, **T** 9267 2900. *Fri and Sat lunch, Tue-Sat dinner. Map 3, C3, p250* Without doubt one of Sydney's best restaurants. Chef Tetsuya Wakuda is world famous for his Japanese/Mediterranean creations. The restaurant has recently been relocated to new, extremely swish premises. Book in advance and if you can afford it, try the 12-course *degustation* dinner.

$$$ Brooklyn Hotel, corner of George and Grosvenor sts, **T** 9247 6744. *Mon-Fri lunch. Map 2, E4, p248* Renowned for its meat dishes (especially steak) with good efficient service and plenty of inner-city pub atmosphere.

$$$ Botanical Gardens Café, Mrs Macquarie Rd, **T** 9241 2419. *Daily 0830-1800.* *Map 2, F9, p249* Sublime tranquillity amidst the Botanical Gardens, right in the heart of a fruit bat colony. In such a setting it may not be everybody's cup of tea but for naturalists and botanists it's really hard to beat.

$$$ Pavilion on the Park, 1 Art Gallery Rd, The Domain, **T** 9232 1322. *Sun-Fri 1200-1500.* *Map 2, G9, p249* Sitting opposite the Art Gallery, the Pavilion provides the perfect escape from the city centre, offering al fresco dining with an eclectic Modern Australian menu. Perfect for lunch after a tour of the gallery.

$$ Casa Asturiana, 77 Liverpool St, **T** 9264 1010. *Daily, lunch and dinner.* *Map 3, D3, p250* Well known for its Mediterranean (Spanish) cuisine and its tapas in particular. Lots of atmosphere and regular live music.

$$ Paddy McGuire's, corner of Kent St and Erskine St, **T** 9212 2111. *Daily, lunch from 1100.* *Map 2, G3, p248* New, spacious establishment, full of character, and offering good pub-grub and fine beers with the ever-popular Irish edge.

$-$$ Hyde Park Café, corner Elizabeth and Liverpool Sts, **T** 9264 8751. *Daily 0700-1630.* *Map 3, D5, p250* Situated in a great spot for escaping the crowds. Good for breakfast, light lunches, coffee and people watching. Being still within earshot of the inner-city traffic it is however a little noisy.

$-$$ MOS Café, corner of Bridge and Phillip St, **T** 9241 3636. *Mon-Fri from 0700, lunch and dinner, Sat and Sun 0800-1800.* *Map 2, E6, p249* A firm favourite located below the Museum of Sydney offering a congenial relaxed atmosphere and imaginative, value Modern Australian. It even offers porridge for breakfast.

Lunch on the Bounty

The most nostalgic and sedate way of cruising the harbour is on board the beautiful Bounty, a fully functional, scale replica of the famous 18th-century tall ship, used in the film of the same name, starring Australia's most famous actor Mel Gibson. Her mooring is in Campbell's Cove, opposite the Opera House, and whether there or out on the harbour she is the most attractive vessel to grace the water. There are a number of daily and special weekend cruise options including lunch, dinner, buffet lunch, pre-dinner and Sunday brunch. The weekday 2-hour Lunch Sail departs at 1230 (from $65) and the Dinner Sail at 1900 (from $99). On Saturday the 2½-hour Buffet Lunch Sail departs at 1230 (from $95), the 1½-hour Pre-Dinner Sail (from $53) at 1600 and the 2½-hour Dinner Sail (from $99) at 1900. On Sunday times are as Saturday except for the 1½-hour Brunch Sail (from $53) departing at a very congenial 1000. Visit or call 29 George Street, The Rocks, T 9247 1789, www.thebounty.com.au

$-$$ Vivo, 388 George St, **T** 9221 1169. *Mon-Fri 0700-2100. Map 2, H4, p249* Right in the heart of all the inner city action offering a refreshingly wide choice at affordable prices. Good coffee.

Darling Harbour and Chinatown

$$ Bodhi Vegetarian Restaurant, Ground Floor, Capitol Sq, George St, **T** 9212 2828. *Daily 1000-1700. Map 3, E4, p250* Considered one of the best places in town for Asian/vegan cuisine. Its Yum Cha is almost legendary. No nonsense service and good atmosphere.

★ Restaurants with a view

- Forty One, Chiefly Tower, (City Centre), p148
- Sydney (Centrepoint) Tower Restaurants, p56
- Quay Restaurant, (Circular Quay), p146
- Wharf Restaurant, Walsh Bay (The Rocks), p147
- Doyle's on the Beach, (Watson's Bay), p162

$$ Chinta Ria-The Temple of Love, Roof Terrace, Cockle Bay Wharf, 201 Sussex St, **T** 9264 3211. *Daily, lunch and dinner. Map 3, B2, p250* With a name like that who can resist? Great aesthetics, good value, and a buzzing atmosphere with quality Malaysian cuisine. Seafood is recommended and good for family groups.

$$ Emperor's Garden BBQ, 213 Thomas St, **T** 9281 9899. *Daily 0900-0100. Map 3, F3, p250* A reliable choice, usually bustling and particularly well known for its duck and suckling pig dishes. The decor is classically tacky, but with such a bombardment of tastes and value for money, who cares?

$$ Emperor's Garden Seafood, 96 Hay St, Haymarket, **T** 9211 2135. *Daily 0800-0100. Map 3, E3, p250* One of the most reliable of the Chinatown restaurants. Always bustling, offering great service and great value for money. But if you're a member of the World Wildlife Fund don't even think about it.

$$ Kam Fook Seafood Restaurant, Level 3, Market City, Hay St, Haymarket, **T** 9211 8988. *Mon-Fri 1000-0100, Sat and Sun 0900-0100. Map 3, E3, p250* A huge establishment and the epitome of Chinatown, great for claustrophobics and for seafood, but not for the faint hearted, or the vegetarian.

$-$$ Blackbird Café, Mid Level, Cockle Bay Wharf, **T** 9283 7385. *Daily 0800 until late. Map 3, B2, p250* Deservingly popular, congenial, laid back and good value, with a huge selection from pasta to steak. Also good for that leisurely (hangover) breakfast.

$-$$ Coast, Roof Terrace, Cockle Bay Wharf, Darling Park, 201 Sussex St, **T** 9267 6700. *Mon-Fri and Sun lunch, daily dinner. Map 3, B2, p250* Offers a fine range of Modern Australian dishes and has a formal, yet relaxed atmosphere and great views across Darling Harbour. Great spot for lunch. Modern Australian with a Mediterranean edge.

$ Dickson House Food Court, corner of Little Hay and Dixon Sts. *Daily 1000-2200. Map 3, E3, p250* A wealth of cheap Asian take-aways with generous but uninspiring counter meals for under $6.

City West: Glebe to Parramatta

$$$ Boathouse on Blackwattle Bay, Ferry Rd, Glebe, **T** 9518 9011. *Tue-Sun lunch and dinner. Map 4, C3, p252* A quality up-market (yet informal) seafood restaurant offering refreshingly different harbour views than those sought at Circular Quay and Darling Harbour. Here you can gaze upon the lights of Anzac Bridge or the comings and goings of Sydney's fishing fleet while tucking in to the freshest seafood.

$$$ Darling Mills, 134 Glebe Point Rd, Glebe, **T** 9660 5666. *Fri lunch , daily dinner. Map 4, G3, p252* Gracious, well-appointed sandstone restaurant with an imaginative Modern Australian menu, open fires and plenty of charm. A fine escape from city buzz.

$$ Flavour of India, 142A Glebe Point Rd, Glebe, **T** 9692 0662. *Sun-Thu 1800-2230, Fri-Sat 1730-2330. Map 4, F3, p252* Quite simply Glebe's best Indian restaurant with lots of character, great service and value for money. Tandoori dishes recommended.

$$ Le Kilimanjaro, 280 King St, Newton, **T** 9557 4565. *Mon-Sat lunch and dinner*. Friendly place, offering authentic, good-value African cuisine even without the couscous.

$$ Steki Taverna, 2 O'Connell St, Newtown, **T** 9516 2191. *Wed-Sun dinner*. Popular and lively Greek restaurant especially well known for its live entertainment. Friday nights are the best, but book ahead.

$$ Thai Pothong, 294 King St, Newtown, **T** 9550 6277. *Tue-Sun lunch, daily dinner*. On a street with more Thai restaurants than chopsticks, the Thai Pothong stands head and shoulders above the rest. Value, choice and good service.

$$ Toxteth Hotel, 345 Glebe Point Rd, Glebe **T** 9660 2370. *Daily from 1100*. *Map 4, E2, p252* A modern, spacious, traditional Australian pub serving mountainous plates of good pub grub.

$-$$ Iku, 25A Glebe Point Rd, Glebe, **T** 9692 8720. *Mon-Fri 1130-2100, Sat and Sun 1130-2100*. *Map 4, H5, p252* The first of what is now a chain of fine vegetarian and macrobiotic vegan cafés under the 'Iku' banner, offering a delicious array of options that have put paid to the rabbit food myth.

$-$$ Tamana's, 169 King St, Newton, **T** 9519 2035. *Daily, lunch and dinner*. Offers reliable no-nonsense Indian diners with great value for money. Eat in or take-away.

$-$$ Thanh Binh, 111 King St, Newtown, **T** 9557 1175. *Thu-Sun lunch, daily dinner*. Good-value Vietnamese. Delicious dishes from simple noodles to venison in curry sauce.

★ **Places for breakfast**

Best

- Sejuiced Café, Bronte (City East), p163
- Sean's Panorama, Bondi (City East), p162
- Zinc, Potts Point (City East), p157
- Fishcafe, Newtown (City West), p155
- Hyde Park Café, (City Centre), p150

$-$$ Badde Manors, 37 Glebe Point Rd, Glebe, **T** 9660 3797. *Daily 0730-late. Map 4, H5, p252* Something of an institution in Glebe for many years, this favourite student café hangout can always be relied on for atmosphere and character, which is more than can be said for the service.

$-$$ Cinque, 261 King St, Newtown, **T** 9519 3077. *Daily 0730-late.* Popular, modern café next to the Dendy Cinema and a small bookshop, which adds to the attraction. Great all day breakfasts and good coffee. Local favourite.

$-$$ Fishcafe, 239 King St, Newtown, **T** 9519 4295. *Daily 0730-2300.* A charming little café decked out with strings of garlic and dried flowers and interesting bits and bobs. Definitely one of Newtown's best and most popular haunts, especially for breakfast and good coffee, but it can be a nightmare getting a seat.

$-$$ Well Connected, 35 Glebe Point Rd, Glebe, **T** 9566 2655. *Daily 0700-2400. Map 4, H5, p252* One of the city's first internet cafés. Laid-back with a whole floor upstairs full of sofas dedicated to surfing the web. The kind of place where a tea break accidentally turns in to a day off. Not a bad cup of coffee either.

Eating and drinking

City East: Kings Cross to Bondi

Kings Cross and Woolloomollo

$$$ Manta Ray, 7 The Wharf, Cowper Wharf Rd, Woolloomooloo, **T** 9332 3822. *Mon-Fri lunch, daily dinner. Map 2, G10, p249* Classy (and expensive) seafood restaurant, some Sydney gourmands say one of the best in the city. Overlooking a flotilla of extravagant launches backed by the city skyline and the Sydney Tower.

$$$ Otto, 8 The Wharf, Cowper Wharf Rd, Woolloomooloo **T** 9368 7488. *Tue-Sun 1200-1500 and 1800-2300. Map 2, G10, p249* Very trendy, quality Italian with an imaginative menu which is thriving in the conglomerate of restaurants that are the focus of the new Woolloomooloo Wharf renovations. Exquisite seafood pastas and all the necessary trimmings, including and some very extrovert waiters.

$$ Bayswater Brasserie, 32 Bayswater Rd, Kings Cross, **T** 9357 2177. *Mon-Thu 1700-2300, Fri 1200-2300, Sat 1700-2300. Map 2, C12, p249* Always a reliable choice attracting a mixed crowd. Sydney suits bring non-Sydney suits here to experience Kings Cross style and unabashed cheek. Immensely popular for its laid-back, yet classy atmosphere, aesthetics and its imaginative Modern Australian cuisine. Seafood, especially oysters, a speciality.

$$ Macleay Street Bistro, 73 Macleay St, Potts Point, **T** 9358 4891. *Daily 0700-late. Map 2, H12, p249* Well-established local favourite. Classy decor and good value, with a wide-ranging blackboard menu. A convivial air, especially at the weekend.

★ **Best**

Leichhardt's Italian espressos

- Bar Italia, 169 Norton Street.
- Sorriso, 70 Norton Street.
- Elio, 159 Norton Street.
- Café Corso at the Italian Forum.
- Frattini, 122 Marion Street.

$$ Shimbashi Soba on the Sea, 6 The Wharf, Cowper Wharf Rd, Woolloomooloo, **T** 9357 7763. *Daily 1100-2200. Map 2, G10, p249* A fine, good-value Japanese restaurant that adds to the choice and quality to be found on the Wharf strip. Mix of pure Japanese cuisine with more familiar meat and poultry dishes.

$$ Zinc, 77 Macleay St, **T** 9358 6777. *Daily, 0700-late. Map 2, H12, p249* Trend-setting and not everybody's cup of tea but there is no denying its increasing popularity, especially for breakfast. Good blackboard menu and friendly service.

$ Govinda's 112 Darlinghurst Rd, Kings Cross, **T** 9380 5155. *Daily from 1800. Map 3, D11, p251* Restaurant and cinema combo offering a great-value, all-you-can-eat vegetarian buffet along with the movie ticket.

$ Harry's Café de Wheels, Cowper Wharf, Woolloomooloo. *Sun-Thu 0700-0200, Fri and Sat 0700-0300. Map 2, H10, p249* An oasis of informality, character and value for money, backed by the trendy, expensive options of The Wharf, Harry's is something of a Sydney institution, offering the famously yummy pies with pea toppings and gravy. One is surely never enough, as the photos of satisfied customers can testify.

Eating and drinking

$ Orange Thai, corner Hughes and Macleay St, **T** 9358 5666. *Daily 1100-2300. Map 2, A12, p249* Cheap and cheerful (and clean) Thai eatery, right in the heart of Kings Cross and perfect for pre-club munchies.

$ Café Hernandez, 60 Kings Cross Rd, Kings Cross, **T** 9331 2343. *24 hrs. Map 2, C12, p249* Great, eccentric 24-hour café serving Spanish fare, great coffee and with a relaxed atmosphere and an interesting clientele ranging from exasperated taxi drivers to last night's failed Don Juans.

Darlinghurst, Paddington and Surry Hills

$$$$ Buon Ricordo, 108 Boundary St, Paddington, **T** 9360 6729. *Fri-Sat lunch , Tue-Sat dinner. Map 3, E12, p251* Lively Italian that enjoys a city-wide reputation offering pasta at its very best. Beautifully presented dishes served with a confidence that this will probably not be your only visit. Bookings essential.

$$$$ MG Garage, 490 Crown St, Surry Hills, **T** 9383 9383. *Mon-Fri lunch , Mon-Sat dinner. Map 3, H8, p251* An ambience that complements the class of the pricey cars that surround the tables. Delightful and imaginative Modern Australian cuisine, but it is certainly a memorable experience. Book ahead.

$$$$ Salt, 229 Darlinghurst Rd, Darlinghurst, **T** 9332 2566. *Mon-Fri lunch , daily dinner. Map 3, D10, p251* Classy establishment with a clientele to match. Can be a bit stuffy and though you get some of the best Modern Australian in the city, you pay for it. Booking is essential.

$$ Bill's, 433 Liverpool St, Darlinghurst, **T** 9360 9631. *Daily breakfast and lunch 0730-1500. Map 3, E11, p251* One of the city's top breakfast cafés with legendary scrambled eggs. Small, and at times overcrowded, but that's all part of the experience.

$$ **Bill's 2 the sequel**, 359 Crown St, Surry Hills, **T** 9360 4762. *Daily breakfast , Mon-Sun 1200-1500 lunch, Mon-Sat 1800-2200 dinner. Map 3, H8, p251* Sister establishment to the above and an equal in popularity, choice and atmosphere. Can get too busy at times.

$$ **Billy Kwong**, 3/355 Crown St, Surry Hills, **T** 9332 3300. *Daily from 1800. Map 3, H8, p251* A small establishment, decked with Chinese antiques and crammed with seating creates a relaxed atmosphere. Great value make this a fine choice for Chinese, especially seafood and duck dishes.

$$ **Fishface**, 132 Darlinghurst Rd, Darlinghurst, **T** 9332 4803. *Daily dinner. Map 3, E10, p251* The best base for fish and other seafood in and around the inner east. Excellent fish and chips but often crammed and noisy.

$$ **Fuel**, 476 Crown St, Surry Hills, **T** 9383 9388. *Daily from 0800, breakfast, lunch and dinner. Map 3, H8, p251* Little sister to the unusual and popular MG Garage restaurant, offering more affordable but equally good bistro-style cuisine. Especially popular for weekend brunch. How does champagne sausage and oysters sound?

$$ **Go Bungai**, 8 Heeley St, Five Ways, Paddington, **T** 9380 8838. *Wed-Sun from 1200 lunch, Tue-Thu and Sun 1800-2000, Fri and Sat 1800-2300 dinner. Map 3, G12, p251* Fine little Japanese restaurant with a loyal following, yet nicely set off the beaten track. A secluded courtyard adds to its appeal.

$$ **Oh, Calcutta**, 251 Victoria St, Darlinghurst, **T** 9360 3650. *Fri lunch, Mon-Sat dinner. Map 3, E11, p251* An award-winning Indian

restaurant: the best in the inner east and the closest you will get to the real thing in Sydney. First rate curries blessed with just the right amount of spice to bombard the tastebuds. Cosy and great value. Book ahead.

$$ **Le Petit Creme**, 118 Darlinghurst Rd, Darlinghurst, **T** 9361 4738. *Daily from 0800. Map 3, D11, p251* Superb little French number with all the classics, from baguettes to cavernous bowls of café au lait. Great omelettes for breakfast or lunch.

$$ **Orphee**, 210 Oxford St, Paddington **T** 9360 3238. *Mon-Sat 1000-around 1800, Sun 0800-around 1800. Map 3, H12, p251* A well-established French-style restaurant considered one of the best in the city, offering a lovely homely atmosphere and imaginative menu. Popular as much for its decor, layout and ambience as its cuisine. Go early to enjoy a pre-dinner drink in the sumptious lounge upstairs.

$$ **Royal Hotel**, 237 Glenmore Rd, Paddington, **T** 9331 5055.*From 1200, lunch and dinner.* One of the best choices at the increasingly popular Five Ways crossroads in Paddington. A grand old pub with gracious yet modern feel. Excellent Modern Australian cuisine is served upstairs in the main restaurant or on the prized veranda. Perfect for a lazy afternoon.

$ **Bar Coluzzi**, 322 Victoria St, Darlinghurst, **T** 9380 5420. *Daily 0500-1900. Map 3, D11, p251* A well-established café that consistently gets the vote as one of Sydney's best. The extended opening hours, the cosmopolitan clientele and the great coffee are the biggest draws as opposed to the food. Great place to go first thing to ease that nefarious 'Cross' hangover.

$-$$ **Café Centaur**, 19 Oxford St, Paddington **T** 9560 3200. *Daily 1000-2330. Map 3, G10, p251* A pleasant, quiet little café in a great bookshop that will delay your tourist wanderings for hours. Light fare, delectable sweets and good coffee.

$ Hot Gossip, 438 Oxford St, Paddington **T** 9332 4358. *Daily 0730-late*. A well-established 'Paddo' café with retro 50s furnishings and an interesting clientele. Good food, healthy smoothies (not just the customers) and a great cakes selection.

$ Indian Home Diner (Paddington), 86 Oxford St, **T** 9331 4183. *Daily 1100-late. Map 3, G11, p251* You really can't go wrong here with the usual great-value (if mild) Indian combo dishes and on this occasion, a small courtyard out back. Try a large butter chicken, then try getting the stains off your t-shirt.

$ Prasit's Thai Takeaway, 395 Crown St, **T** 9332 1792. *Tue-Sun lunch and dinner. Map 3, H8, p251* Great-value Thai restaurant and take away and the locally recommended cheap option in Surry Hills. Don't automatically expect to get a seat however. Plenty of vegetarian options.

$ Mickey's Café, 268 Oxford St, Paddington, **T** 9361 5124. *Daily 0900-late. Map 3, H12, p251* Local favourite with a huge range of value options from burgers to burritos. Quick, convenient and especially good for lunch.

$-$$ Una's, 340 Victoria St, Darlinghurst, **T** 9360 6885. *Daily 0730-late. Map 3, D11, p251* Local favourite offering generous hangover cure breakfasts and European-influenced lunches, including schnitzel and mouth-watering strudel. A nice change in a city obsessed with complicated gastronomic combinations.

Further east

$$$$ Doyle's on the Beach, 11 Marine Parade, Watson's Bay, **T** 9337 2007. *Daily, lunch and dinner.* Sydney's best-known restaurant, Doyle's has been in the same family for generations and has an unfaltering reputation for superb seafood, an ideal location, atmosphere and harbour/city views that all combine to make it a one of the premiere dining experiences in the city. Book well ahead and ask for a balcony seat. Sunday afternoons are especially popular. You could combine the trip with a walk around the heads.

$$$ Hugo's, 70 Campbell Parade, Bondi Beach, **T** 9300 0900. *Daily dinner, Sat and Sun breakfast and lunch.* *Map 6, H2, p253* A well-established favourite in Bondi, offering a combination of classy atmosphere, quality Modern Australian cuisine and fine views across the beach.

$$$ Sean's Panorama, 270 Campbell Parade, Bondi Beach, **T** 9365 4924. *Sat and Sun lunch, Wed-Sat dinner.* *Map 6, F6, p253* Another Bondi classic, set at the southern end of the beach, away from the confusion and mayhem of the strip. Modern Australian with a European edge. Especially popular for breakfast.

$$ Aqua Bar, 266 Campbell Parade, Bondi Beach, **T** 9130 6070. *Daily 0630-1530.* *Map 6, F6, p253* Healthy options, laid-back atmosphere. The view and excellent breakfasts make the Aqua a big favourite in Bondi.

$$ Watson's Bay Hotel, 1 Military Rd, Watson's Bay, **T** 9337 4299. *Daily, lunch and dinner.* Next door to Doyles is this more casual affair offering equally good views of the city skyline and a superb outdoor barbecue area offering a range of fresh seafood. You can even cook your own. Great for a whole afternoon especially at the weekend.

$-$$ Coogee Bay Hotel, corner of Coogee Bay Rd and Arden St, Coogee, **T** 966-5000. *Daily from 1100.* The most popular spot in Coogee day or night with multiple bars, huge open air eating, value pub grub and live entertainment. The 'action' is more remarkable than the food.

$-$$ Le Paris-Go Café, 38 Hall St, Bondi, **T** 9130 8343. *Daily 0700- 1700. Map 6, F4, p253* Bohemian, laid back and popular, with good healthy vegetarian options and generous all-day breakfasts.

$-$$ Love in a Cup, 106 Glenayr Ave, Bondi Beach, **T** 9365 6418. *Mon-Sat 0700-1700, Sun 0800-1700. Map 6, F2, p253* A well-kept café secret in Bondi, off the beaten track and popular with locals, especially for breakfast/brunch. Good value and good coffee.

$-$$ Sejuiced, 487 Bronte Rd, Bronte, **T** 9389 9538. *Daily 0700- 1830.* Has competition on both sides, but is consistently the café of choice on the 'Bronte strip'. Favourite breakfast spot at weekends and a great start (or finish) to the cliff-top walk between Bronte and Bondi.

City North: Manly to Northern Beaches

$$$$-$$ Bathers Pavilion, The Esplanade, Balmoral Beach, **T** 9969 5050. *Daily from 0700.* Ideally located in the historic pavilion overlooking Balmoral Beach, superb spot for breakfast, lunch and dinner, with quality of food to match. Café or fine dining options. Great choice after a day spent on Balmoral beach, or for those wanting a quiet escape.

$$$ Watermark, 2A The Esplanade, Balmoral Beach, **T** 9968 3433. *Daily from 0800.* Set in a beautiful location overlooking a beautiful beach, Watermark is well off the beaten track, but a gem, offering great Modern Australian with a seafood speciality. Also good for breakfast.

$$ Alhambra, 54 West Esplanade, Manly, **T** 9976 2975. *Daily, lunch and dinner. Map 5, D2, p253* A refreshing change from fast food and Modern Australian, the Alhambra offers Spanish and Mediterranean fare, with tapas, naturally, being a speciality.

$$ Armstrong's, Manly Wharf, **T** 9976 3835. *Daily, lunch and dinner. Map 5, E2, p253* Well positioned on the wharf overlooking the beach and divorced from the many fast food joints along the Corso. Good-value Modern Australian and locally recommended.

$$ Bower Restaurant, 7 Marine Parade, **T** 9977 5451. *Daily breakfast and lunch, Thu and some weekends dinner. Map 5, E6, p253* Located right at the end of Marine Parade with memorable views back towards Manly Beach. Great spot for breakfast.

$$ Brazil, 46 North Steyne, Manly, **T** 9977 3825. *Daily from 0800 until late. Map 5, C4, p253* Set right in the heart of the action overlooking Manly Beach. Standard Modern Australian and good coffee, but gets a bit busy in the evenings.

$$ Out of Africa, 43 East Esplanade, Manly **T** 9977 0055. *Mon-Sun dinner, Thu-Sun lunch. Map 5, E3, p253* Good value, authentic African cuisine. Oddly out of place in Manly, but refresh- ingly different, even attracting residents from across the water.

$-$$ Mosman RSL, 719 Military Rd, **T** 9969 7255. *Daily lunch and dinner.* Offers three levels including a great-value restaurant and al fresco bistro overlooking the main street and across the city.

Choice of à la carte, pub food, or cook your own barbecue. Live entertainment at weekends.

$-$$ Mosman Yacht Club, opposite the Mosman Ferry Terminal, **T** 9969 1244.   A little-known option with club prices in a setting overlooking the marina and properties you probably couldn't afford. The lamb shanks are excellent.

Blue Mountains

$$$ Silk's Brasserie, 128 The Mall, Leura, **T** 47842534.   *Daily lunch and dinner.   Map 8, E3, p255*   Popular modern restaurant, considered to be the best in Leura, offering Australian cuisine and plenty of atmosphere. Book ahead.

$$$ Solitary, 90 Cliff Dr, Katoomba, **T** 47821164.   *Sat, Sun and public/school holidays lunch, Tue-Sat dinner.   Map 8, E3, p255*   Classy award winner with a fine reputation offering imaginative Modern Australian cuisine and fine views across the Jamieson Valley.

$$ Arjuna, 16 Valley Rd, Katoomba, **T** 47824662.   *Thu-Mon from 1800.   Map 8, E3, p255*   The best Indian restaurant in the region and the views are almost as hot as the curry. Book ahead.

$$ Cleopatra, 118 Cleopatra St, Blackheath, **T** 47878456. *Tue-Sun dinner, Sun lunch.   Map 8, E3, p255*   Primarily a guesthouse but the very classy French-style has won so many awards for its cuisine; it is often dubbed the 'restaurant with accommodation'. Expensive but worth it.

$$ Mount Tomah Botanical Gardens Restaurant, Bells Line of Road, **T** 45672154, www.rbgsyd.nsw.gov.au   *Daily 1000-1600. Entry to gardens $6.   Map 8, B5, p255*   Although the gardens are well worth visiting in their own right, it is the views, the short walks and the restaurant that make a visit extra special.

$$ **The Savoy**, 26 Katoomba St, Katoomba, **T** 47825050. *Daily 1100-2000. Map 8, E3, p255* Locally recommended for value and especially for its conventional and kangaroo steak dishes.

$ **Paragon**, 65 Katoomba St, Katoomba, **T** 47822928. *Daily 0800-1700. Map 8, E3, p255* If you have a sweet tooth you just cannot afford to miss out on an art-deco Katoomba institution.

$ **Vulcans**, 33 Govett's Leap Rd, Blackheath, **T** 47876899. *Fri-Sun lunch and dinner. Map 8, D2, p255* Well-known Blackheath institution offering superb coffee and great affordable meals. The only drawback is the limited opening hours.

Hawkesbury River Region

$$$Settlers Arms, 1 Wharf St, St Albans, **T** 4568 2111. Superb 1830s historic pub with its tiny stone-floored bar, ideal for lunch. See also p142 for accommodation details.

$$$ **Wellum's Lake Guesthouse**, Lot 1 Wellum's Lake, Settlers Rd (3 km south of St Albans), **T** 4568 2027, **F** 4568 2027, cbr@ix.net.au A great café overlooking Wellum's Lake. See also p142 for accommodation details.

Sydney has some fine pubs in both the city centre and suburbs to suit most tastes. Most are the traditional, street corner Australian Hotels, but there are lots of modern, trendy establishments, pseudo Irish pubs and historic alehouses on offer. Unlike Europe, generally speaking, you will find that most antipodeans do not buy 'rounds'. So beware, don't suddenly offer your group of new friends a tray full of pints expecting to get the kind offer returned. They will just think you're an exceptionally nice foreigner who's had too many and has got lots of spare cash to throw around. Many pubs, especially those along Oxford Street and in Kings Cross, attract a lively, happy and cosmopolitan mix of straight and gay clients. The best drinking area in Sydney is probably The Rocks, where history, atmosphere and, most importantly, darn good beer combine for a great night out. Opening hours vary but most bars and pubs in Sydney with live entertainment stay open into the small hours, especially at weekends. Quieter establishments usually call last orders as early as 2230.

Although the main focus for travellers, particularly backpackers, Kings Cross is not necessarily the best nightlife area in town. True, a great night out (and certainly an experience) is on offer, but recent drug busts in some clubs have given the place a slightly dodgy edge. There are quite a few popular clubs, most of which keep entry costs down to attract the backpacker crowd.

For the latest in club information and special events get the free *3-D World* magazine, available in many backpackers, cafés or clubs themselves, www.threedworld.com.au. Other useful sites include www.sydney.sidewalk.com.au or www.sydney.cityserach.com.au

Circular Quay and The Rocks

Bars

Australian Hotel, 100 Cumberland St, **T** 9247 2229. *Map 2, C4, p248* Wedged on a street corner and one of The Rocks most popular bars. Fine range food and al fresco seating. A must in any Rocks pub crawl.

Lord Nelson, 19 Kent St, **T** 9251 4044. *Map 2, B2, p248* The Nelson is Sydney's oldest pub and within its hallowed, nautically themed stone walls, it brews its own ales and also offers some fine pub grub and accommodation. Get there early to secure a seat. The only drawbacks are its propensity to close when the night is still young and the price of the beer. A place for conversation as opposed to live entertainment.

Orient, 89 George St, **T** 9251 1255. *Map 2, C3, p248* An old favourite set in the heart of Sydney's oldest precinct. Good range of beers and a good atmosphere but can get too busy at weekends and late at night.

Hero of Waterloo, 18 Lower Fort St, **T** 9252 455 *Map 2, B3, p248*
Can be a bit of a squeeze but is full of character and always
entertaining. No-nonsense service and good beer. Pitched
somewhere between a locals' haunt and a tourist venue.

Mercantile, 25 George St, **T** 9247 3570. *Map 2, B4, p248* The
pseudo Irish tavern, the Merc is often busy, pretty wild and offers a
fairly decent pint of Guinness, as well as great live traditional music
until late. Usually the place everyone ends up on a Rocks pub crawl
with some inebriated soul on stage with the band, playing the
tambourine and blowing bubbles.

Clubs

Jacksons on George, 176 George St, **T** 9247 2727. *Mon-Fri
0800-0500, Sat 0600. $15. Map 2, D4, p248* Huge club spread over
four floors with five bars, dining, dancing, live bands and pool.

City Centre: the CBD

Bars

Scruffy Murphys, corner Gouldburn St and George St, **T** 9211
2002. *Open well in to the wee hours. Map 3, E4, p250* A popular,
well-established, yet rather tired, Irish pub that always draws the
crowds. It's a great place to meet people, the live bands and beers
are good, but there really is very little Irish about it.

Paddy McGuires, Corner of George and Hay, **T** 9212 2111. *Map 3,
F4, p250* An Irish-themed establishment that has been refurbished
and offers pleasant surrounds in which you can actually have a
decent conversation or sample a fine range of beers. The pub food is
good and there is live entertainment most nights.

Scubar, corner Rawson Pl and Rawson Lane, **T** 9212 4244, www.scubar.com.au *Map 3, F3, p250* A popular backpacker-orientated pub that offers cheap beer, pizzas, pool, big TV screens and popular music until late.

Clubs

Slip Inn, 111 Sussex St, **T** 9299 4777. *Open daily, free entry before 2200. Corner of Sussex St and King St. Map 2, H3, p248* A trendy night spot with three rooms and a courtyard that fills with the young and beautiful, who let rip to a mix of house and rave. Good Vibrations on a Saturday is especially popular.

Globe, corner Park St and Elizabeth St, **T** 9264 4844. *Sun-Thu 1100-2200, Fri and Sat 1100-0600. Fri $10, Sat $15. Map 3, B5, p250* The place to go if you like funk and are indeed funky.

Gas, 477 Pitt St, Haymarket, **T** 9211 3088. *Daily 2200-0400. $15-25. Map 3, E4, p250* The unfortunately named Gas is one of the best venues for dance music in the city with excellent, clued-up DJs revving up the crowds to a range of soul, funk, hip-hop, house and R&B, especially on Fridays and Saturdays.

Civic Hotel, 388 Pitt St, **T** 8267 3181. *Open nightly. Under $10. Corner Gouldburn St. Map 3, E4, p250* A noted pub, cocktail bar and restaurant, the Civic is a traditional weekend haunt for a cosmopolitan crowd who repeatedly come to enjoy old anthems and classics.

! Sydney Pub Trek is a very messy backpacker-based pub-crawl on Thursday nights with plenty of price reductions, from $25, T 9235 0999. But don't expect a deep conversation on the political situation in Afghanistan.

Darling Harbour and Chinatown

Bars

Cargo Bar, 52-60 The Promenade, **T** 9262 1777. *Map 2, G1, p248*
Laid back and popular, especially for an extended pub lunch.

Ettamogah Bar, Harbourside Shopping Complex, Cockle Bay,
T 9281 3922. *Map 3, A1, p250* A distinctly gimmicky Aussie
offering with lots of cartoon style decor. Not everyone's pint of
lager and a bit rowdy at times.

Cohibar, Shop 359, Harbourside, Darling Harbour, **T** 9281 4440.
Map 3, A1, p250 A classy place popular with city suits and trend
setters. On two levels with a terrace and cocktail lounge, this is a
great place to enjoy a cigar and/or the view across Cockle Bay.

Clubs

Home, 101 Cockle Bay Wharf, **T** 9266 0600. *Daily 2200-0600. $15.*
Map 3, A2, p250 One of the country's largest state of the art nightclubs. On four levels you will find lots of skin tight pants and boob
tubes getting on down to a vibe of mainly house and trance. Every
Saturday there is an enjoyable kinkidisco.

Cave Nightclub, Star City Complex, Pirrama Rd, **T** 9566 4755.
Fri and Sat 2200-0600, Sun 2130-0500. Southwest of Pyrmont Bay.
Very trendy establishment offering good dance and R&B combo,
but don't go unless your dayglo pants are in this month's colour.

Goodbar, 11A Oxford St, **T** 9360 6759. *Wed-Sat 2200-0300. From
$15. Map 3, 7D, p251* A well-established club and an old favourite

amongst Sydneysiders, from the sexy young things to the sexually confused and the odd forgotten-how-to-be-sexy fossils. Mixed music and good value.

Arq, 16 Flinders St, **T** 9380 8700. *Mon-Thu free, Fri, Sat, Sun from 2200, from $15.* *Map 3, F9, p251* A new club with two large dance floors, plenty of space and a good balcony from which to watch a friendly crowd of both straight and gay.

City East: Kings Cross to Bondi

Bars

Albury Hotel, 6 Oxford St, Paddington, **T** 9361 6555. *Until 0400.* *Map 3, F10, p251* More an experience in debauchery than a bar and a firm favourite with the gay community, yet still welcoming a mixed and diverse crowd. The drag queens frolic, the beer flows and the music pumps well in to the wee hours. If you're single and confused, you won't be for long.

Bourbon and Beefsteak, 24 Darlinghurst Rd, Kings Cross, **T** 9358 1144. *24 hrs.* *Map 3, B12, p251* Large American-style pub and eatery conveniently open all hours and as a result attracting all types in all stages of inebriation.

Coogee Bay Hotel, 9 Vicar St, Coogee, **T** 9665 0000. Multiple bars and live music, beachside, this is the focus of Coogee nightlife, but has a good atmosphere both night and day.

Durty Nelly's, 9 Glenmore Rd, Paddington, **T** 9360 4467. *Last orders 2330.* *Map 3, C12, p251* The smallest, the best and most intimate Irish pub in the city with a grand congenial jam session on Sunday evenings.

Best

★ **Beer and character**

- Paddy McGuire's, corner George and Hay (City Centre), p150
- Lord Nelson (The Rocks), p169
- Lord Dudley (Paddington), p175
- Durty Nelly's (Paddington), p182
- Friend In Hand (Glebe), p176

Grand Pacific Blue Room, Paddington, **T** 9331 7108. *Corner Oxford and South Dowling Sts. Map 3, F10, p251* Cool lounge bar popular with a mixed crowd. Live entertainment and funky cocktails.

Hard Rock Café, 121 Crown St, Kings Cross, **T** 9331 1116. *Map 3, C8, p251* Complete with the suspended automobiles, electric guitars and band memorabilia that have now been the trademark of the global outlets for 30 years. Roll in for two-for-one drinks, Mondays to Fridays, 1700-1900.

Hotel Bondi, 178 Campell Pde, Bondi, **T** 9130 3271. *Map 6, G3, p253* A lively bar, popular with the surf set and backpackers, with live bands and a nightclub attached.

Kings Cross Hotel, 248 William St, Kings Cross, **T** 9358 3377. *Remains open well in to the small hours. Map 3, C11, p251* A spacious, rowdy backpacker favourite with a weird interior in the shadow of the huge Coca Cola sign.

Kitty O'Sheas, 384 Oxford St, Paddington, **T** 9360 9668. *Map 3, H12, p251* A large mainstream Irish pub, very popular especially at weekends when live bands get the feet tapping and the beer spilling. If you need to escape the melee or have a white shirt on, try the bar upstairs.

Lord Dudley, 236 Jersey Rd, Paddington, **T** 9327 5399, www.lorddudley.com.au *Last orders 2330. Deep in the Paddington suburbs on the fringe with Woollahra.* A grand historic rabbit warren looking much like a traditional olde English Pub with beer to match. There is also some great, if expensive pub-grub on offer.

O' Malley's Hotel, 228 William St, Kings Cross, **T** 9357 2211. *Last orders around 0200. Map 3, C11, p251* The local Irish offering with good live bands, but no means the best Irish pub in the city. Live entertainment at weekends.

Royal Hotel, Glenmore Rd, Paddington, **T** 9331 2604. *Crossroads with Goodhope and Heeley Sts.* A large atmospheric public bar downstairs and a fine restaurant on the second floor. Excellent both day and night with a good selection of beers.

Woolloomooloo Bay Hotel, 2 Bourke St, Kings Cross, **T** 9357 1177. *Map 2, H10, p249* Aussie-style establishment with Karaoke nights and regular DJs. When you can no longer pronounce the name of the place it is definitely time to go home.

Clubs

Icebox, 2 Kellet St, Kings Cross, **T** 9331 0058. *2200-0500. From $5-15, free on Mondays. Map 3, C12, p251* Offers more hardcore house and rave than most clubs in The Cross.

World, 24 Bayswater Rd, Kings Cross, **T** 9357 7700. *Daily. $5 after 2200. Map 3, C12, p251* Newly refurbished laid back club set in grand historic surrounds and offering mainly UK house music and funk. Hosts some of the city's finest DJs.

Zen, 22 Bayswater Rd, Kings Cross, **T** 9358 4676. *Daily 2000-0500. From $15. Map 3, C12, p251* A revamped venue, located next to

World. As the name suggests, this time it is an Oriental theme that is the gimmick. It concentrates on progressive house music. Friday nights are especially good.

City West: Glebe to Parramatta

Bars

Friend In Hand Pub, 58 Cowper St, **T** 9660 2326. Looks more like a venue for a international garage sale, but oozes character and also offers a bar café and Italian Restaurant. The Cockatoo does bite.

Toxteth Hotel, 345 Glebe Point Rd, **T** 9660 2370. More modern, traditionally Australian affair. It is always pretty lively, has pool competitions and serves mountainous plates of good pub grub.

From arias in the Opera House to giant chess in Hyde Park, there is always a wealth of things to entertain in Sydney, 24 hours a day, 365 days a year. For the latest information and reviews check the *Metro* section in the Friday *Sydney Morning Herald*. *The Beat* and the *Sydney City Hub* are free weeklies, readily available in restaurants, cafés, bars and bookshops in and around the city centre. On the net try www.sydney.sidewalk.com.au   The usual ticket agent is *Ticketek*, Sydney Entertainment Centre, Harbour Street, Haymarket T 9266 4800, www.ticketek.com.au   They produce their own monthly events magazine, *The Ticket*. Ticketmaster, T 136100 also deal with theatre tickets. Discounted tickets can often be secured on the same day from *Halftix*, Darling Park, 201 Sussex Street, T 9286 3310. Bookings can also be made over the net, www.halftix.com.au   For cinema listings see the *Sydney Morning Herald* or call Movieline, T 9218 2421.

Cinema

The biggest cinema attraction (literally) in Sydney is the huge eight-storey-high IMAX Theatre in Darling Harbour (see p69). In the city centre most of the major cinema complexes are to be found along George Street between Town Hall and Chinatown.

Chauvel, corner Oxford St and Oatley Rd, **T** 9361 5398. *Map 3, H12, p251* A showcase for more retro, foreign or fringe films.

Hayden Orpheum Cinema, 180 Military Rd, Cremorne, **T** 9908 4344. *From $13, children $10. Often half-price Tue.* A wonderful art deco cinema on the North Shore that offers a fine alternative to the modern city cinemas.

Moonlight Cinema, Centennial Park, **T** 1900 933 899, movies@moonlight.com.au *23 Nov-23 Feb. Map 1, p251* Older classics under the stars. Take a picnic and plenty of cushions.

Comedy

National or international comedy is generally hosted by smaller theatres, like the Lyric and The Belvior (see Performing Arts, below).

Club Luna, the Basement, 29 Reiby St, **T** 9251 2797. *From $13. Map 2, E5, p248* Excellent on Sunday nights.

Exchange Hotel, corner Beattie and Mullins sts, Balmain **T** 98106099. *Wed. From $5.* A number of city hotels, including the Exchange, have comedy nights once a week.

Comedy Store, Bent St, Fox Studios, **T** 9357 1419. *Tue-Sat. From $10-27.*

Laugh Garage, first floor, Macquarie Hotel, corner Gouldburn St and Wentworth Ave, **T** 9560 1961. *Thu-Sat. $11-22. Map 3, E6, p250.*

Comedy Cellar, 1 Bay St, Ultimo, corner of Broadway and Bay St, **T** 9212 3237.

Gambling

Gambling is big business in Australia with an estimated $10-12 billion being spent annually. Given the population of 19 million that figure makes Australians the most avid gamblers on earth. You will find that almost every traditional Australian hotel and pub in Sydney has the omnipresent rows of pokies (slot machines).

Star City Casino, 80 Pyrmont St, a coin's roll from Darling Harbour, **T** 9777 9000, www.starcity.com.au *Open 24 hrs.* Smart casual dress mandatory. The main focus for trying your luck in Sydney is a vast arena with 200 gaming tables, 1,500 pokies and lots of anxious faces. Perhaps the best thing to do is just take a look inside then throw a coin and make a wish in the splendid water features that front the Star City complex.

Music

Rock

Tickets for a major international band will cost anything from $60 to $90. The three main concert venues are massive and modern.

Metro, 624 George St, **T** 9287 2000. *Map 3, D4, p250.*

Sydney Entertainment Centre, 35 Harbour St, City, **T** 9320 4200. *Map 3, E2, p250.*

Sydney SuperDome, Homebush Bay Olympic Park, **T** 8765 4321, www.superdome.com.au *Map 7, E3, p254*.

Jazz

For daily details of jazz gigs tune in to the **Jazz Gig Guide** at 0800 on *Jazz Jam*, 89.7FM, Eastside Radio, Monday to Friday. The **Sydney Jazz Club** can be contacted on **T** 9798 7294. Major venues include the following.

The Basement, 29 Reiby Pl, Circular Quay, **T** 9251 2797, www.thebasement.com.au *Map 2, E5, p248*. **Harbourside Brasserie**, Pier One, The Rocks, **T** 9252 3000. *Map 2, A4, p248*. **Soup Plus**, 383 George St, **T** 9299 7728. *Map 2, G4, p248*.

Australian

You will almost certainly hear the bizarre and extraordinary tones of the didgeridoo somewhere during your explorations, among the buskers on Circular Quay or in the many souvenir shops in the city.

Australia's Northern Territory and Outback Centre, 28 Darling Walk, Darling Harbour. *Tue-Sun 1300, 1500 and 1700*. Live performances of the didgeridoo and other traditional Aussie instruments.

Didj Beat Didjeridoo Shop, Clocktower Square Mall, **T** 9251 4289. *Map 2, C4, p248* A great venue to hear impromptu performances by staff.

Reds Australian Restaurant, 12 Argyle St, The Rocks, **T** 9247 1011. *Map 2, c4, p248* Daily performances with dinner, 1745 and 1930.

Blues

Zambezi Blues Room, 481 Kent St, **T** 9266 0200. *Behind Town Hall Square.* *Map 3, B3, p250*   A fine venue and free.

Folk

All the Irish pubs offer folk jam nights early in the week and live bands from Wednesday to Sunday.

Durty Nelly's, 9-11 Glenmore Rd, **T** 9360 4467. *Off Oxford St.* *Map 3, C12, p251* A more intimate Irish pub offering low-key jam sessions on Sunday afternoons.

Mercantile Hotel, 25 George St, The Rocks. *Map 2, B4, p248* Some of the best folk in town.

Scruffy Murphys, corner Gouldburn St and George St, **T** 9211 2002. *Map 3, E4, p250*   A busy venue.

Classical music

Whether it is an evening listening to the **Australian Chamber Orchestra**, **T** 9357 4111, or the **Brandenburg Orchestra**, **T** 9363 2899, in one of the great venues' mighty auditoria (including the **Opera House**, see below and p41, the **Town Hall**, see p58, and the **St Andrew's Cathedral**, see p58), or in a variety of less high-profile locations around the city, from cathedrals to city parks, there is always something on.

The annual **Sydney Festival** in January traditionally hosts a number of classical music events including the very popular and congenial **Symphony in the Park** and **Opera in the Park** held in the Domain. For listings consult the *Metro* section of the *Sydney*

Morning Herald, www.metro.citysearch.com.au or the City Council's events website, www.sydneycity.nsw.gov.au

The principal ticketing agency is **Tiketek**, **T** 9266 4800, www.ticketek.com.au There are a number of outlets in the city including the Theatre Royal Sydney, MLC Centre, 108 King Street, or the City Recital Hall (see below). Bookings can be made on-line.

City Recital Hall, Angel Place, Pitt St, between Hunter and King sts, **T** 8256 2222, www.cityrecitalhall.com.au *Map 2, G5, p248*.

Sydney Conservatorium of Music, Royal Botanical Gardens, Macquarie St, **T** 9351 1342, www.usyd.edu.au/su/conmusic *Map 2, E7, p249* Free student recitals every Friday at 1310 during term.

Sydney Opera House, box office **T** 9250 7250, www.soh.nsw.gov.au *Prices from about $28-180. Map 2, B8, p249 See also p41* The Opera House's Concert Hall is Sydney's largest classical music venue and home to both the **Sydney Symphony Orchestra** and **Opera Australia**.

Performing arts

Sydney Opera House, box office **T** 9250 7250, www.soh.nsw.gov.au *Prices from about $28 to $180. Map 2, B8, p249 See also p41* Naturally the focus for the performing arts in Sydney, the Opera House offers five venues, the Concert Hall, the Opera Theatre, the Drama Theatre, the Playhouse and the Studio, all presenting a diverse range of performances. The Opera House is the home of the **Australian Ballet** and the **Sydney Dance Company**. The Drama Theatre is a performing venue for the **Sydney Theatre Company** while the Playhouse is used for small-cast plays, lower-key performances, lectures and seminars. The Studio is used for contemporary music and performance.

Belvoir Theatre, 25 Belvoir St, in the south of Surry Hills, **T** 9699 3444.   A good range of performances in a lesser-known venue.

Capitol, 13 Campbell St, **T** 9320 5000.   *Map 3, E4, p250*   A diverse range of performances in a lovingly restored space.

Lyric Theatre and the **Showroom**, Star City complex, 80 Pyrmont St, southwest of Pyrmont Bay, **T** 9777 9000.   Theatre, concerts, comedy, dance and musicals from around $40-80 for a major performance.

State Theatre, 49 Market St, **T** 19022 62588, www.statetheatre. com.au   *Map 3, A4, p250*   A dynamic range of specialist and mainstream performances and cinema.

Sydney Entertainment Centre, 35 Harbour St, **T** 9320 4200.   *Map 3, E2, p250*   One of the city's largest and most modern performance venues, hosting a wide selection of acts and shows.

Theatre Royal, MLC Centre, 108 King St, **T** 136166.   *Map 2, H4, p248*   Noted for its musicals and plays.

Wharf Theatre, Pier 4/5, Hickson Rd, Walsh Bay, **T** 9250 1700.   *Behind the Scenes tours are available, $5.*   *Map 2, A3, p248*.   **Base for Bangarra**, **T** 9251 5333, www.bangarra.com.au, an exciting contemporary Aboriginal dance group who also perform at the Opera House. Also secondary home for the **Sydney Theatre Company** and other performance groups.

As Australia's largest and most vistited metropolis, Sydney offers a variety of festivals and events to rival any major city in the world. The highest-profile of the annual festivals is the Gay and Lesbian Mardis Gras which has, since its foundation in 1978, grown to become the most spectacular event of its kind on the planet. But it is not all pink boob tubes and leather cod pieces: Sydney can offer something for everyone from surf fests to sonnets. The remarkably diverse list of events fit in to three main categories: sports, culture and the arts, with the added spice of an invariably colourful take on international or national celebrations like the fireworks display at New Year, or the annual Australia Day celebrations, both of which are centred around the perfect backdrop of the harbour and Circular Quay. The following is a summary of the major festivals held annually, or those major events specific to 2003/4. For comprehensive listings check out the free *This Month in Sydney* booklet from the VIC, the weekend *Sydney Morning Herald* and the website www.sydneycity.nsw.gov.au

January

New Year Every New Year kicks in with spectacular fireworks and celebrations that centre around The Rocks and the Harbour Bridge. Other good vantage points include Milsons Point, The Opera House and Cremorne Point.

The Sydney Festival and Fringe Festival Taking place through most of the month, this is a celebration of the arts including the best of Australian theatre, dance, music and visual arts and is held at many venues throughout the city. For many the highlight are the free open-air concerts in the Domain, including Opera in the Park and Symphony under the Stars, www.sydneyfestival.org.au

Australia Day (26th) Annual celebrations with the focus being a flotilla of vessels flying the flag on the harbour, www.australiaday.com.au

February

Gay and Lesbian Mardi Gras Festival and Parade Without doubt the most famous Sydney event is this legendary festival held each February for a month. It is an opportunity for the gay community to celebrate, flaunt their being, entertain and shock. The highlight is a good shake of the pants and cod pieces (or very lack of them) during the spectacular parade from Liverpool Street to Anzac Parade held at the end of the festival. **T** 9557 4332, www.mardigras.com.au

March

The Royal Agricultural Easter Show Held every Easter and now uses the facilities at Olympic Park as a venue.

Fire and water

Sydney's streets and harboursides become even livelier than usual during its festivals, especially Mardi Gras, which has become a major global party event.

April

Anzac Day (25th) The annual dawn service at the Martin Place Cenotaph and a parade down George Street.

May

Sydney Morning Herald Half Marathon For the fit the half marathon is a great attraction, especially when it involves crossing the Harbour Bridge.

Australian Fashion Week Celebrations showcasing some of the country's top designers. There is also another fashion week in November to preview the best of the winter collections.

June

Sydney Film Festival Crunching of popcorn at a two-week fest for film buffs featuring over 150 features from 40 countries, **T** 9660 3844, www.sydneyfilmfestival.org.au

August

Sun-Herald City to Surf Increasingly popular and far less soporific than watching the big screen, this is a 14-km race from Bondi Beach to the City Centre, **T** 1800 555 514.

September

Festival of The Winds September sees the Festival of The Winds at Bondi Beach which is a colourful festival of kites and kite flying, while the avid sports fans fight over tickets and take several days drinking leave for the Rugby League and Rugby Union Grand Finals.

Manly Arts Festival Based around the Manly Art Gallery and Museum (see p94), the Manly Arts Festival has blossomed into one of the State's best community-based arts festivals, encompassing film, theatre, kids' and busking events, www.manly.nsw.gov.au/v artsfestival

---

October

Manly Jazz Festival The annual weekend Manly Jazz Festival is a gathering of Australia's best along with some fine foreign imports. Stages located in several public arenas including the beachfront and the Corso, as well as hotels, restaurants and bars, **T** 99771088.

2003 Rugby World Cup The 2003 Rugby World Cup kicks off in Sydney at the Telstra Stadium and venues around the country.

November

Sydney to the Gong Activity is the highlight once again with the 80 km Sydney to Wollongong cycle race. For details contact *Bicycle NSW*, **T** 9283 5200, www.ozemail.com.au/~bikensw

---

December

Carols by Candlelight Over Christmas, Carols by Candlelight is the main festive public celebration of song in the Domain.

Bondi Beach Christmas Party (25th) The wild and wicked grab a beer glass and a patch of sand here and the party usually ends up as a mass streak in to the waves.

Sydney to Hobart Race (26th) Far more serious, though no less chilly on the flotation devices, is this sailing race, which departs the inner harbour, winds allowing, every Boxing Day.

Whether it's top international fashion labels or jewellery, open-air markets or seafood, Sydney can offer a superb shopping experience. In the city, most of the large department stores, arcades, malls and specialist boutiques are along George Street and in the area around Pitt Street Mall, Castlereagh Street and King Street. Not to be missed is the magnificent Queen Victoria Building (QVB), which is a vast and historic edifice in which the levels of retail therapy are almost legendary. Nearby, connecting George Street with Pitt Street is the smaller, yet no less attractive and historic, Strand Arcade, T 9232 4199, www.strandarcade.com.au, built in 1892. The largest of the suburban malls is the Warringah Mall, Pittwater Rd, Brookvale, North Shore, T 9905 0633. The suburbs of Newtown (Kings Street) and Glebe (Glebe Point Rd) have fascinating shops selling everything from cod pieces to secondhand surfboards. Double Bay, Mosman and Paddington (Oxford Street) are renowned for stylish boutique clothes shops and The Rocks is definitely the place to go for a didgeridoo or cuddly koala.

Most shops' opening hours are from 0900-1730 on weekdays. Thursday is late-night shopping until 2100. At the weekend, shops may shut one or two hours early. Sales are generally held in January and June. For more information on Sydney shopping pick up the comprehensive *Sydney Shopping, The Official Guide* from the VIC, call the City Info Line, **T** 9265 9007, or visit the website www.sydney-shopping.com.au

Aboriginal art

There have been disturbing stories in recent years surrounding the authenticity of Aboriginal art and methods with which some, even reputable dealers, commission art from Aboriginal artists. This has allegedly included the practice of paying artists a few tins of beer in return for works of art, which are then sold on for thousands of dollars, none of which the artist will ever see. If you intend to buy original Aboriginal art ask plenty of questions that relate to the work's authenticity and look out for the *National Indigenous Arts Advocacy Association Label of Authenticity*. The *Traveller Consumer Helpline*, **T** 1300 552 001, can also help.

Aboriginal and Tribal Art Centre, 1st Floor, 117 George St, The Rocks, **T** 9247 9625. *Daily 1000-1700. Map 2, C5, p248*.

Coo-ee Emporium and Aboriginal Art Gallery, 98 Oxford St, Paddington, **T** 9332 1544. *Mon-Sat 1000-1800, Sun 1100-1700. Map 3, E8, p251*.

Gavala Aboriginal Art Centre, Shop 377, Harbourside, Darling Harbour, **T** 9212 7232. *Map 3, A1, p250*.

Hogarth Galleries, 7 Walker Lane, **T** 9360 6839. *Map 3, F12, p251*.

Australiana

From the iconic **Akubra** hats (minus the gimmick of corks) and **RM Williams** boots to the **Driza-Bone** oilskin coats, you'll find all the main brands and outlets in Sydney. Generally speaking these world-famous brands and products are beautifully made and well worth the money. For example a pair of 'RMs' will, provided you look after them, last a lifetime. For a good range of souvenir products the many outlets in The Rocks (and weekend **Rocks Market**) are a good source.

RM Williams, www.rmwilliams.com.au, Shop 1-2 Chiefly Plaza, on the corner of Hunter and Phillip Sts. *Map 2, G6, p248*.

Goodwood Saddlery, 237-239 Broadway, Southeast of Wentworth Park, **T** 9660 6788. *Mon-Fri 0900-1730, Thu until 2000, Sat 0900-1700, Sun 1000-1600*. Akubra hats, Drizabones and – should you have a horse in tow – a fine range of saddlery, can be all be found here.

Craft Australia Boutique, 4th Floor, *David Jones* department store, 65 -77 Market St, **T** 9266 6276. *Map 3, A5, p250* For unique Australian crafts.

Object, 3rd Floor, Customs House, 31 Alfred St, **T** 9247 9126, www.object.com.au *Near Circular Quay*. *Map 2, E6, p248* A showcase of the best in authentic Australian crafts.

Australia's Northern Territory and Outback Centre, 28 Darling Walk, Darling Harbour, **T** 9283 7477, www.outbackcentre.com.au Souvenirs and gifts.

Bookshops

Dymocks, 428 George St, **T** 1800 688 319, www.dymocks.com.au *Mon-Wed and Fri 0900-1800, Thu 0900-2100, Sat and Sun 0900-1700. Map 2, H4, p248* The largest bookshop in Australasia is the major player and there are other outlets throughout the city (350 George Street, 261 George Street, and 34 Hunter Street).

Travel Bookshop, 175 Liverpool St, **T** 9261 8200. *Mon-Fri 0900-1800, Sat 1000-1700. Map 3, D6, p250* For travel guides and maps, but also a good source of information.

Gleebooks, 49 Glebe Point Rd, **T** 9660 2333, www.gleebooks.com.au *Mon-Sun. Map 4, G5, p252* A smaller, more traditional bookshop. A sister **Gleebooks** shop, selling secondhand and children's books, is down the road (number 191).

Sappho Books at 165 Glebe Point Rd, **T** 9552 4498. *Mon-Sun 1000-2200. Map 4, G5, p252* A good independent bookshop.

Berkelouw's Books, 19 Oxford St, Paddington, **T** 9360 3200. *Open until late. Map 3, G11, p251* A great range of secondhand books with the added attraction of a café.

Goulds Book Arcade, 32 Kings St, Newtown. This lost world is the largest and most bizarre secondhand bookshop in the city. If Sophia Lauren ran out the door followed by a posse of neolithic men you'd hardly bat an eyelid.

Clothes

You will find all the major international labels in Sydney with most having outlets in the major city centre shopping streets, arcades and department stores. **Oxford Street** in Paddington and the suburbs of **Double Bay,** and, to a lesser extent, **Chatswood**, are renowned for their boutique clothes stores and Australian designer labels. Names and labels to look for include *Helen Kaminski*, *Collette Dinnigan, Morrissey, Bare, Isogawa* and *Bettina Liano*. For designer bargains try the **Market City** above Paddy's Markets in Haymarket.

If you are looking for something completely different: perhaps a pair of pink hot pants or fluffy ear muffs, then head for **Kings Street** in Newtown. For the keen clothes shopper it will be impossible to leave the place empty-handed and who knows, it may change your wardrobe and style forever.

Contemporary fine art

There are many art galleries showcasing some of the best Australian contemporary artists with most being in **The Rocks** or **Paddington**. Try to get hold of the free *Art Find* brochure from one of the galleries or the Sydney VIC. **Ken Done** is one of the most famous Sydney-based artists. He has a colourful, almost childlike style which you will either love or hate.

Ken Done Gallery, 123 George Street, The Rocks, **T** 92472740. www.gallery@done.com.au *Map 2, C5, p248*.

Department stores

On or near Market Street are three great Sydney institutions: the department stores of **Grace Bros**, **David Jones** and **Gowing Bros**.

Grace Bros, 436 George St, **T** 9238 9111, www.gracebros.com.au *Map 3, A4, p250*.

David Jones, 65-77 Market Street, **T** 9266 5544, www.davidjones. com.au *Map 3, A5, p250*.

Gowing Bros, 319 George St, **T** 9287 6394, www.gowings.com.au *On the corner of Market Street and George Street. Map 3, A5, p250.*

Didgeridoos and boomerangs

Didj Beat Didgeridoo Shop, Clocktower Square Mall, The Rocks, **T** 9251 4289, www.didjibeat.com.au *Daily 1000-1830. Map 2, C4, p248* You can purchase didgeridoos and boomerangs all over the city but this is perhaps the best outlet. There are over 2,000 'didjies' on show and the staff are delighted to pass on their impressive playing skills. A free one-hour workshop is offered with your purchase (from $55-1500) and they also stock a good selection of original Aboriginal art.

Factory outlets

Birkenhead Point Outlet Centre, Roseby St, Drummoyne, **T** 91813922. *West of the centre.* A vast outlet for straight-from-the-factory bargains.

Food and wine

For a taste of Australian foods take a look at the food hall in the elegant **David Jones** (see Department stores, above).

Even if you don't like seafood a trip to the **Sydney Fish Markets**, Pyrmont is fascinating with the shoal of stalls setting up their displays of Australia's best from about 0800 (see p66).

For late-night food shopping the **Coles Express** supermarkets, on the corner of George and King Streets, at the Wynard Station and in Kings Cross, are open daily, 0600-2400.

Australian Wine Centre, 1 Alfred St, Circular Quay, **T** 9247 2755, www.wine.ptylimited.com.au *Daily. Map 2, D5, p248* Whether you are a novice or a seasoned wine buff, before purchasing any

Shopping

Australian labels you might benefit from a trip here. The staff are very knowledgeable and are backed by a great collection of over 1,000 wines. They also offer a worldwide delivery service.

Jewellery

Given the fact Australia produces over 90% of the world's **Opals** it is not surprising to find a wealth of specialists dealing in their almost surreal beauty and worth. To ensure authenticity and good workmanship only purchase opals from retailers who are members of the *Australian Opal and Gem Industry Association Ltd* (AOGIA) or the *Jewellers Association of Australia*.

Pearls from the great Australian *pinctada maxima* oyster, ranging from gold to snow white, are also big business.

Flame Opals, 119 George St, **T** 9247 3446, wwwflameopals. com.au *Mon-Fri 0900-1845, Sat 1000-1700, Sun 1130-1700. Map 2, C5, p248.*

Opal Minded, 36-64 George St, **T** 9247 9885. *Daily 1000-1800. Map 2, B5, p248.*

Australian Opal Cutters, Suite 10, 4th Floor, 250 Pitt St, **T** 9261 2442. *Map 3, B5, p250.*

Gems from the Heart, Shop 33 in the QVB, George St, **T** 9261 2002. *Map 3, A/B4, p250.*

Bunda, Shop 42, Ground Floor, QVB, George St, **T** 9261 2210. *Map 3, A/B4, p250* Some of the best and biggest pearls.

Markets

There are plenty of weekend markets held in the inner city that offer an eclectic and colourful range of new and secondhand clothes, arts, crafts and foods.

The **Sydney Fish Markets** are a fascinating experience held every morning in Pyrmont (see p66).

The Rocks Market, George St, The Rocks. *Sat and Sun at the top end of George St. Map 2, B5, p248* Sydney's most popular market, this is supplemented on Sundays with an uncluttered open-air market on the Opera House concourse, concentrating mainly on arts, crafts and souvenirs.

Paddy's Markets, Haymarket. *Thu-Sun. Map 3, F2, p250* The biggest market in the city centre is gloomy and fairly tacky.

Paddington Market, 395 Oxford St. *Sat, in the grounds of a church.* Good inner-suburbs market.

Balmain Market, St Andrews Church, Darling St, on the corner of Darling St and Curtis St. *Sat.*

Glebe Market, grounds of Glebe Public Schools, Glebe Point Rd. *Sun. Map 4, H4, p252.*

Bondi Markets, Campbell Pde. *Sun. Map 6, G3-F4, p253.*

Outdoor

Kent Street is the place to start looking for camping and outdoor equipment. **Paddy Pallin, Mountain Equipment** and **Patagonia** are all within a guy-rope of each other. For **Rent- A-Tent** outlets, **T** 998-74924 in Hornsby Heights, or **T** 9653 1631 in Galston.

Paddy Pallin, 507 Kent St, **T** 9264 2685,
www.paddypallin.com.au *Map 3, C3, p250.*

Mountain Equipment, 491 Kent St, **T** 9264 5888,
www.mountainequipment.com.au *Map 3, A/B4, p250.*

Patagonia, 497 Kent St, **T** 9264 2500. *Map 3, A/B4, p250.*

Adventure Sports Australia, 722 George St, **T** 9281 6977.
Map 3, E3, p250.

Photography

Ken Duncan Gallery, George St, The Rocks (opposite the VIC).
Map 2, C5, p248 For some excellent panoramic Australian
photographs check out this Rocks gallery.

Peter Lik Gallery, the QVB, George St, www.peterlik.com.au
Map 3, A/B4, p250 Another good source of Australian photography.

Sport and fitness is part of the national psyche in Australia and the most successful sportsmen and women are afforded the same celebrity and financial status as film stars in the United States, or pop stars in Great Britain. Although Melbourne boasts many of the high-profile national and international sporting events (including the Grand Prix and Australian Tennis Open), Sydney offers some stiff opposition. Domestic rugby league also has a huge following in the city, culminating with the national Grand Finals. In summer international test cricket is the main feature, while in winter rugby union tests and 'Super 12' matches are held at the Telstra Stadium, just one of several superb sporting venues that are the legacy of the 2000 Olympic Games. Even without any special events, these facilities are still worth seeing, and there's plenty of scope for breaking into a run (or surf or sail or skate or sky dive) yourself.

Australian rules football

Sydney Cricket Ground (the SCG), Moore Park, Paddington , T9380 0383, www.sydneycricketground.com.au *Tours available Mon-Fri at 1000 and 1300, Adult $19.50, child $13, family $52. South of Paddington.* In winter the SCG is taken over by the Sydney Swans, www.sydneyswans.com.au, and their fanatical local following.

Cricket

Sydney Cricket Ground (the SCG, see above for details), is a legendary venue for national and international cricket matches. Cricket has an almost religious following in Australia, and this, plus the SCG's reputation, makes a day spent there watching a test or a one-day international cricket match a memorable experience. You will also find there is as much entertainment off-field as on.

Diving

Sydney offers some surprisingly good diving. The southern beaches, La Perouse and the Botany Bay National Park are the best spots. There are many dive shops in the city and several companies offering tuition and trips, including the popular Dive Centre.

Dive Centre, 10 Belgrave St, Manly, **T** 9977 4355. *Map 5, C3, p253* and 192 Bondi Rd, Bondi, **T** 9369 3855, www.divesydney.com Shore, boat and shark dives from $40 (own gear), $80 (hire) and Open Water Certificates from $270.

Fishing

Despite all the harbour activity, both the fishing and the water quality in Sydney Harbour is said to be pretty good, with species like flathead, whiting and trevally regularly caught, especially

Tours and tickets

Test Rugby, Aussie Rules and Test Cricket match tickets are often hard to come by. A ticket will cost from $40-70 for a cricket test match and $40-$100 for a rugby Grand Final. The usual ticket agent is **Ticketek**, T 9266 4800, www.ticketek.com.au If you cannot secure tickets or don't rate your chances securing a spare ticket outside the venue (often possible), joining the throngs of Sydneysiders in the city pubs can be just as enjoyable and atmospheric.

Tours of the SCG, SFS, T 9380 0383, and Telstra, T 8765 2300, Stadiums are available to the public.

downstream from the Harbour Bridge. Offshore, the fishing improves dramatically and Sydney is home to its own fishing fleet that regularly catch such exotic species as marlin and tuna.

Charter One, Manly, T 04 0133 2355, www.charterone.com Trips range from a $65 three-hour jaunt to a $125 full-day, including tackle hire.

Fitness/gyms

Cook Phillip Park Aquatic Centre, 6 College St, T 9326 0444. *Next to Hyde Park in the CBD. Map 3, B7, p251* An impressive centre and one of the most accessible.

Inline skating

Inline skating is especially popular along the beachfronts of Manly and Bondi, in Centennial Park and around Farm Cove in the Botanical Gardens. Hire will cost you about $11 per hour with $6 extra for every hour after that or around $20 for all-day hire.

Action Inline, Shop 3/93-95 North Steyne (corner Pine St), Manly, **T** 9976 3831, www.action-skate.com.au *Map 5, A3, p253*.

Bondi Boards and Blades, 148 Curlewis St, Bondi, **T** 9365 6555. *Map 6, F2, p253*.

Total Skate, 36 Oxford St, **T** 9380 6356. *Near Centennial Park. Map 3, D7, p251*.

Rugby union and league

Telstra Stadium, Olympic Park, Homebush Bay, **T** 8765 2300, www.stadiumaustralia.com.au *Map 7, E3, p254* The main focus of national and international rugby union, rugby league and soccer matches. Sadly, given its size it has lost the atmosphere that was such a feature of the former venue, the Sydney Football Stadium. For information on union in Australia visit www.rugby.com.au

Sailing

The fickle waters of Sydney Harbour host a number of events, the most noted being the start of the **Sydney to Hobart** race every Boxing Day. 6-m sailing skiffs take part in the **Formula One** races every weekend from October to April.

Sydney Flying Squadron, **T** 9955 8350 (Sat), or the **Australian Sailing League**, **T** 9363 2995 (Sun). Join a spectator ferry that follows the Formula One races.

Sydney by Sail, National Maritime Museum, **T** 9280 1110. Introductory 1½ sailing lessons from $54.

Sea kayaking

Sea kayaking is a great way to see cruise the harbour and explore the backwaters and bays of the inner suburbs. The Middle Harbour, branching off between Middle Head and Clontarf, snakes over 10 km to the lesser-known North Shore suburbs and offers a quiet environment with wildlife. Prices start at $15 per hour or $70 per day.

Sydney Harbour Kayaks, 3/235 The Spit Rd, Mosman **T** 9960 4389, info@4shk.com Guided trips and kayak rental.

Q.Craft, Shop 3, 200 Pittwater Rd, Manly, **T** 9976 6333. Manly rental outlet.

Country Road Adventures, **T** 1300 130 561, www.countryroad.net.au Excellent guided day-trips up the vast Hawkesbury River harbour from $120 (includes pick-up).

Sky diving

Simply Skydive, CM12, Mezzanine, Centrepoint, City, **T** 9231 5865, info@simplyskydive.com.au Test your courage in and around Sydney from $265.

Surfing

Surfing is a major national sport and Sydney's ocean beaches are a year-round venue. Triathlons and Surf Lifesaving competitions are also a regular feature of the sand and surf. The best spots are Bondi and Manly but most of Sydney's beaches offer great possibilities. www.wavecam.com.au has up-to-date surf conditions.

Manly Surf School, North Steyne Surf Club, Manly Beach, **T** 9977 6977, www.manlysurfschool.com *Map 5, B4, p253* Good value daily classes from 1100-1300. From $45 for one lesson. Five days from $150.

Dripping Wet Surf Company, Shop 2/93-95 North Steyne, Manly, **T** 9977 3549. *Map 5, B4, p253* Boards, body boards, flippers and wetsuits for hire. Board hire costs from $12 per hour.

Bondi Surf Company, 2/72 Campbell Pde, **T** 9365 0870. *Map 6, p253*.

Swimming

Sydney Aquatic Centre, Olympic Park, **T** 9752 3666. *Map 7, E3, p254* The primary focus of Australian swimming, consistently the best in the world, is open to the public in 'peacetime'.

Cook Phillip Park Aquatic Centre, 6 College Street, **T** 9326 0444, *$4.50, children $3.30*. *Next to Hyde Park. Map 3, B7, p251* In the centre of town, this centre is impressive not so much due to its modern facilities, but because of its imaginative design and construction under the ground.

Sydney Olympic Pool, Alfred St, Milsons Point, North Shore, **T** 9955 2309. *$3.80, children $1.80*. Offering probably the best view of any swimming pool in Australia, the older Sydney Olympic Pool sits almost below the Harbour Bridge.

Walking

There are many structured well-trodden options in the city but sometimes the best thing to do is to choose a stretch of coast, a suburb or a section of the city centre and just explore. Within the city centre the walk along the **Farm Cove** foreshore from the **Opera House to Macquarie Point** (one hour) is excellent and best done at dawn or dusk. Circular Quay itself is a bombardment of the senses and in either direction from the **Opera House,** past **the Rocks** to **Dawes Point** (two to five hours) or back is always memorable. **Darling Harbour** (two to five hours) during the day, and perhaps more especially at night, is similarly blessed with a wealth of interesting urban architecture and tourist attractions. Other *urban action* walks within the city include a stroll along **Kings Street** in Newtown or along **Oxford Street** and around the quaint suburbs of **Paddington,** with a welcome pint stop in one of the older, traditional pubs. To the east of the city, the scenic oceanside walks from **Watson's Bay** to **the Gap** and **South Head** (two hours) and from **Bondi** to **Bronte** (an hour and a half) are both recommended. **Centennial Park** offers a vast area of parkland tracks and small lakes. On the **North Shore** the walk to **Bradley's Head** (one hour) from **Taronga Zoo** offers lovely city views as well as history and you have the option of carrying on to the views and fortifications of **Middle Head. Manly** to **Spit Walkway** (three to four hours) is another popular track offering great harbour views. **Manly** to **North Head** is another option with the ocean and city views from its terminus being the memorable highlight. At the very terminus of the northern beaches the walk to soak up the views from the **Barrenjoey Head lighthouse** can provide just one highlight of a full-day trip to **Palm Beach**. The **Blue Mountains** offer great walking opportunities outside the city, see p101.

Windsurfing and whitewater rafting

Balmoral Windsurfing and Sailing School, 2 The Esplanade, Balmoral Beach, **T** 9960 5344.   Learn or hire.

Olympic Whitewater Stadium, Penrith (50 km), **T** 4730 4333. *Map 8, F8, p255*   The whitewater rafting sessions make a great day out.

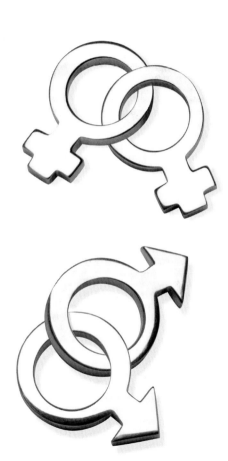

Sydney has a thriving gay and lesbian community that has the identity and panache to match any city in the world. Without doubt the main reason for its near legendary status is the Gay and Lesbian Mardi Gras Festival held every February. The four-week extravaganza is the biggest of its type in the world and offers a wide range of cultural and community events that culminate with a spectacular parade from Liverpool Street to Anzac Parade. Although the event (and the parade in particular) is now immensley popular, congenial and wildly colourful, it took several years after its inception in 1978 as a gay rights protest march to shake off the prejudice and the bigotry that ensued. Even without the festival the gay scene plays a big part in the very fabric of city life with the main focus for social activity being centred around Oxford St, especially at the western end between Taylor Square and Hyde Park, and Newtown, in the inner west. There you will find a conglomerate of clubs and cafés that attract a loyal following with many others attracting a casual mix of both straight and gay.

Mardi Gras

The highlight of the four-week gay and lesbian festival is the spectacular February parade from Liverpool Street to Anzac Parade (at the end of the festival). **T** 9557 4332, www.mardigras.com.au

Information

For more information and venues look out for the free gay papers *Capital Q* (weekly) and the *Sydney Star Observer* available at most gay friendly restaurants, cafés and bookshops, especially along Oxford Street. Useful websites include www.oz.dreadedned.com For accommodation listings try www.qbeds.com.au

The Bookshop, 207 Oxford St, **T** 9331 1103. *Map 3, F9, p251* A good source of gay and lesbian information.

Accommodation

LL-C Manor House Boutique Hotel, 85 Flinders St, Darlinghurst, **T** 9380 6633, **F** 9380 5016, www.manorhouse.com.au *Map 3, H9, p251* Restored Victorian mansion offering 20 period furnished rooms (all en-suite) from standard to luxury with spa. Friendly, congenial atmosphere and well located near to Darlinghurst bars and clubs. Facilities include restaurant, cocktail lounge, plunge pool and internet access. Breakfast included.

LL-L Oxford Koala Hotel, corner of Oxford and Pelican Sts, Darlinghurst, **T** 9269 0645, **F** 9238 2741, www.oxfordkoala.com.au *Map 3, E7, p251* Modern multi-storey, gay-friendly hotel located right in the heart of the action. Wide range of affordable rooms, suites and self-contained apartments, restaurant, bar, pool and secure parking.

C **Wattle Hotel**, 108 Oxford St, Darlinghurst, **T** 9332 4118, **F** 9331 2074, www.sydneywattle.com.au *Map 3, E8, p251* Ideally placed, medium-range boutique hotel offering basic but clean and affordable ensuites some with balconies and fine views of the city.

Bars

Albury Hotel, a firm favourite with the gay community, see p173.

Stonewall Hotel, 175 Oxford St, Darlinghurst, **T** 9360 1963. *Daily 1200-0500. Map 3, E8, p251* One of the liveliest gay venues in the city set on various levels and offering plenty of action and organized events from karaoke and drag shows to regular DJs from Thursday to Saturday. Attracts a young crowd, straight and gay.

Newtown Hotel, 174 King St, Newtown, **T** 9557 1329. *Daily 1100-2400 (2230 Sun).* Attracts a friendly crowd of both gay men and lesbians in the heart of Newtown's happening King Street. Free drag shows most nights.

Nightclubs

Midnight Shift, 85 Oxford St, Darlinghurst, **T** 9360 4319. *Daily 1200-0500. Map 3, E8, p251* Well-established, large, multi-level club especially popular with gay men. Congenial mixed bar and an excellent dance venue.

DCM, 33 Oxford St, Darlinghurst, **T** 9267 7036. *Fri and Sat (times vary according to events). Map 3, E7, p251* Large and immensely popular weekend venue with drag shows and some of the best dancing and DJs in the city. Cover charge varies. Welcomes both straight and gay. Be prepared for queues.

Sydney is eminently child-friendly, provided you don't let them out of your sight. Bear in mind that Australia's largest city is manic, colourful, full of distractions and highly aquatic – all positive, yet at the same time potentially disastrous ingredients. The most obvious attractions for children include Taronga Zoo, The Sydney Aquarium, Australian and Powerhouse Museums and, of course, the city's numerous patrolled beaches. All cater well for the needs and safety of children and just about guarantee a memorable, if exhausting day out. You will also find that hotels and restaurants generally welcome children, with the exception perhaps of some of the most expensive that aspire to provide for the more sedate demands of the corporate market or couples. It pays to make enquiries prior to booking. For further information on kids' Sydney see www.sydneyforchildren.com *Sydney for the Under-Fives* by Seana Smith (ISBN 0330362488, $22) is also useful for those with toddlers and is available at most major bookshops in the city.

Beaches and swimming

Sydney's glut of patrolled beaches are the ideal venue for kids, but counsel them on safety and swimming between the flags. **Bondi** (see p85), **Manly** (West Esplanade, see p91), **Balmoral** (see p90) and **Coogee** (see p86) are all good, safe options for children, with many having man-made pools. Sydney's copious public swimming pools are another option with the **Sydney Olympic Pool** (see p209) at Milsons Point offering parents the added attraction of superlative views of the harbour bridge. The **Cook Phillip Park Aquatic Centre** (see p206) next to Hyde Park is within walking distance of most inner-city hotels.

Entertainment

IMAX Theatre, Darling Harbour, **T** 9281 3300, www.imax.com.au *1000-2200, $16.20, children $10.80, family $38, Explorer bus stop 22. Map 3, B2, p250* On the Cockle Bay waterfront, the eight-storey-high cinema is a favourite with older children (see also p69).

Rocks Toy Museum and Puppet Theatre, Kendall Lane, The Rocks, **T** 9251 9793. *Daily 1000–1730. $6, children $4, family $12. Map 2, C5, p248* Housed in the former 1854 Coachhouse the museum boasts over 3,000 toys spanning two centuries. The Puppet Theatre, also located in Kendall Lane, offers free shows at 1100, 1230 and 1400 weekends (daily during school holidays).

Gardens and parks

Royal Botanical Gardens, Mrs Macquarie's Rd via Art Gallery Rd, **T** 9231 8111, www.rbgsyd.gov.au *0700-sunset. Free. Tropical Centre daily 1000-1600, $5. Explorer Bus route, stop 3. Map 2, F8, p249* The Botanical Gardens are worth mentioning for children, not so much for the plants or free space to run around in, but for

Kids

217

the resident colony of bats. The size, number and smell of the fruit bats will doubtless impress (see also p59).

Featherdale Wildlife Park, 217 Kildare Road, Doonside, **T** 9622 1644. *0900-1700 daily. $15, children $7.50, family $38. By car go via the M4 and turn off on to Reservoir Rd. After 4 km turn left on to Kildare Rd. Alternatively take the train from the city (Western Line) to Blacktown then bus 725 from the station. Map 7, D1, p254* Although not in the same league as Taronga, and less accessible, Featherdale is a great venue for kids. The biggest bonus is the fact that many of the most congenial creatures like kangaroos and kookaburras are allowed to roam free within the park providing a better chance for kids to get up close and personal with the animals (see also p77).

Museums

Australian Museum, 6 College St, **T** 9320 6000, www.austmus.gov.au *0930-1700, $8, children $3, family $19, (special exhibitions extra). Explorer Bus route, stop 7. Map 3, C7, p251* Although it may seem rather academic, the Australian Museum near Hyde Park is excellent for children. The *Natural History* section in particular has memorable displays. The *Search and Discovery* section also offers endless hours of hands-on entertainment (see also p59).

Powerhouse Museum, 500 Harris St, Ultimo, **T** 9217 0111, www.phm.gov.au *1000-1700 daily. $10, children $3, family $23. Monorail, LightRail or Sydney Explorer bus stop 17. Map 3, E1, p250* The number, variety and size of the displays at the Powerhouse is guaranteed to impress children with highlights including full-scale trains and aeroplanes (see also p68).

Kids

Zoos and aquariums

Taronga Zoo, Bradley's Head Rd, **T** 9969 2777, tours **T** 9969 2455, www.zoo.nsw.gov.au *0900-1700 daily. Zoo $23, children $12, family $57. Taronga is best reached by ferry from Circular Quay (Wharf 2). Ferries every half-hour Mon-Fri 0715-1845, Sat 0845-1845 and Sun 0845-1730. A Zoo Pass combo ticket which includes ferry transfers and zoo entry costs $28.40, child $14.30. Map 1, p251* The city's most popular draw for children offers hours of entertainment, keeper talks and all the necessary facilities including cafés. Added attractions include the ferry ride from the city centre (a great incentive to eventually leave), a gondola ride above the centre of the park and a highly entertaining free-flight bird show. For teenage kids with a specific interest in wildlife ask about their specialist 'Night Zoo' tours or on-going educational programs (see also p89).

Sydney Aquarium, Aquarium Pier, Darling Harbour, **T** 9262 2300, www.sydneyaquarium.com.au *0900-2000. $23, children $11, family $49 (Aquarium Pass with ferry from Circular Quay, $27.40, child $14.30). Explorer bus stop 21. Map 3, A2, p250* This fascinating mix of entertainment and education is a quality experience for children, with everything from sharks and penguins to seals and platypuses, as well as the more intimate attractions of touch tanks and a discovery centre (see also p62).

Kids

Kids

Directory

Airline offices

(CBD unless otherwise stated) **Aerolites Argentinas,** 580 George St, **T** 1800 222 215; **Air Canada**, Level 12, 92 Pitt St, **T** 9232 5222; **Air China**, Level 11, 115 Pitt St, **T** 9232 7277; **Air Fiji**, Level 5,17 Bridge St, **T** 8272 7889; **Air France**, 64 York St, **T** 9244 2100; **Air New Zealand**, Level 4, 10 Barrack St, **T** 13 2476; **Air Pacific**, Level 10, 403 George St, **T** 9244 2626; **American Airlines**, Mezzanine Level, 141 Walker St, North Sydney, **T** 1300 650 747; **British Airways**, Level 19, AAP Centre, 259 George St, **T** 1300 767 177; **Continental Airlines**, 64 York St, **T** 9244 2242; **Eastern Australia Airlines**, Qantas Airways Domestic Terminal, Mascot, **T** 9691 2333; **Garuda Indonesia**, 55 Hunter St, **T** 9334 9900; **Hazelton Airlines**, Building 305, Eleventh St, Mascot, **T** 13 1713; **Impulse Airlines,** Eleventh St, Sydney Kingsford Smith Airport, Mascot, **T** 9317 5400; **Japan Airlines**, Level 14, 201 Sussex St, **T** 9272 1111; **KLM Royal Dutch Airlines**, 5 Elizabeth St, **T** 1800 505 747; **Lufthansa**, 143 Macquarie St, **T** 9367 3800; **Skimax-Qantas,** Level 3, 263 Clarence St, **T** 9267 1655; **Singapore Airlines**, 17-19 Bridge St, **T** 9350 0100; **Sydney Harbour Seaplanes Pty Ltd**, Lyne Park Rose Bay, **T** 9388 1978; **Thai Airways**, 75 Pitt St, **T** 9251 1922; **United Airlines**, Level 6, 10 Barrack St, **T** 9317 8933; **Virgin Atlantic Airways**, Level 8, 403 George St, **T** 9244 2747.

Airport information

Information on flight arrivals/departures, **T** 9667 6065, www.sydneyairport.com.au

Banks and ATMs

All major bank branches with ATMs are readily available on all principal shopping and eating streets in Sydney, especially along George St.

Bicycle hire

Companies include **Bicycles in the City**, 722 George St, **T** 9281 6977 (offer not only hire but maps and touring information); **Inner City Cycles**, 151 Glebe Point Rd, Glebe, **T** 9660 6605; **Woolly's Wheels**, 82 Oxford St, **T** 9331 2671 and the **Manly Cycle Centre**, 36 Pittwater Rd, Manly, **T** 9977 1189. For general advice contact **Bicycle NSW**, Level 2, 209 Castlereagh St, **T** 9283 5200, www.ozemail.com.au/~bikensw For *Sydney Cycle Ways* maps and additional information contact the **RTA**, **T** 9218 6816**.**

Car hire

All the usual suspects have offices at the airport (Arrivals south) including **Avis**, **T** 9667 0667, **Hertz**, **T** 9669 2444, **Thrifty**, **T** 9317 4161, **Budget**, **T** 132848, **National**, **T** 9207 9409 and **Red Spot**, **T** 9317 2233. In the city try **Avis**, **Budget** and **Ascot** centred on or around William St, Darlinghurst. Cheaper more localised companies include **Dollar**, Sir John Young Crescent, **T** 9223 1444 and **Bayswater Rentals**, 180 William St, Kings Cross, **T** 9360 3622. Rates start from about $55 per day.

Credit card lines

Amex, Level 1, 124-130 Pitt St, **T** 1300 139 060. **Diners**, **T** 1300 360 060. **Mastercard**, 146 Arthur St, North Sydney, **T** 9466 3700. **Visa**, Level 27, 225 George St, **T** 9256 2400.

Consulates

See Embassies, below.

Dentists

After Hours Dental Emergency, 144/313 Harris St, Pyrmont, **T** 9660 3322.

Disabled

The free leaflet *CBD Access Map Sydney,* available from the VICs or information booths, is a useful map and guide for the disabled. For more detailed information contact the *Disability Council of NSW*, **T** 9211 2866 (free call 1800 044 848) or *Disability Services Australia*, **T** 9791 6599, www.dsa.org.au

Doctors
Travellers Medical and Vaccination Centre, Level 7, 428 George St, **T** 9221 7133. The website www.drscef.com.au/surgeries   also has listings throughout the city.

Electricity
The current in Australia is 240/250v AC. Plugs have 2 or 3 blade pins and adapters are widely available.

Embassies
Belgium, 12a Trelawney St, Woollahra, NSW, **T** 02 9327 8377. **Canada**, Level 5, 111 Harrington St, Sydney, **T** 02 9364 3000. **France**, 31 Market St, Sydney, **T** 02 9261 5779. **Germany**, 13 Trelawney St, Woollahra, NSW, **T** 02 9328 7733. **Netherlands**, 500 Oxford St, Bondi Jnc, Sydney, **T** 02 9387 6644. **New Zealand**, Level 10, 55 Hunter St, Sydney, **T** 02 9223 0222. **Sweden**, Level 5, 350 Kent St, Sydney, **T** 02 9262 6433. **Switzerland**, 500 Oxford St, Bondi Jnc, Sydney, **T** 02 8383 4000. **United Kingdom**, Level 16, The Gateway, 1 Macquarie Pl, Sydney, **T** 02 9247 7521. **USA**, 19-29 Martin Pl, Sydney, **T** 02 9373 9200.

Emergency numbers
For **Police**, **Fire brigade** or **Ambulance** dial 000.

Foreign exchange
Foreign exchange is readily available on the arrivals concourse of Sydney Airport. In the city there are many outlets, especially around Circular Quay and along George St; **Thomas Cook**, QVB Walk, Shop 64, **T** 9264 1133; **Visa Customer Centre**, 91 George

St, The Rocks, **T** 1800 180 900 (1000-1800); **American Express**, 124 and 50 Pitt St, **T** 9239 9226/**T** 1300 139 060.

Hospitals
St Vincent's Hospital, Victoria St, Darlinghurst, **T** 9339 1111. **Royal North Shore Hospital**, Pacific Highway, St Leonard's, **T** 9926 7111. **Prince of Wales Hospital**, High St, Randwick, **T** 9382 2222. **Sydney Children's Hospital**, **T** 9382 1111.

Internet/email
Internet is widely available throughout the city centre with the southern end of George and Pitt Sts (between Liverpool and Hay) and the western end of Oxford St (between Crown and College) having numerous outlets. **Global Gossip** have outlets at 34 Wentworth Ave and 770 George St in the CBD and 317 Glebe Point Rd, Glebe. Most backpackers provide their own internet facilities and outlets in the outer suburbs are listed in the relevant text. Expect to pay from $3-8 per hr. Be careful to confirm your start and finish time with the person on duty. Overcharging or convenient 'rounding up' seems to be common.

Laundrettes
City Laundromat, Millennium Tower, corner Sussex and Bathurst sts, **T** 9264 6661.

Left luggage
With the global threat of terrorist attacks left luggage has become a sensitive issue in Sydney. For the most up to date information contact the **VIC**.

Libraries
State Library of New South Wales, Sydney City Library, 456 Kent St, **T** 9265 9470. *Mon-Fri 0800-1900, Sat 0900-1200* (see p53).

Lost property

CityRail, T 8202 2000, Sydney Ferries **T** 9207 3101, also visit www.131500.com.au/lost_property.asp

Media

The main daily newspaper in Sydney is the excellent *Sydney Morning Herald* which has comprehensive entertainment listings daily (especially in the Fri *Metro* section). There are some excellent, free tourist brochures including the *Sydney Official Guide, This Week in Sydney, Where Magazine*, the interesting suburb-orientated *Sydney Monthly* and, for the backpacker, *TNT* (NSW Edition) or the *Backpack Guide to Australia*. For entertainment look out for *The Revolver* and *3-D World*. All these and others are available from the principal VICs, city centre information booths, or from some cafés, newsagents and bookshops. Some of the best Sydney websites include www.visitnsw.com.au, www.sydney.citysearch.com.au and www.discoversydney.com.au

Opticians

Colin Wood, Level 1, 5 Hunter St, CBD, **T** 92332889.

Pharmacies

Crest Hotel Pharmacy, 60A Darlinghurst Rd, Kings Cross, **T** 9358 1822 (open late), **City Pharmacy** and **Chase Medical Centre**, 136 Macquarie St, **T** 9247 2390.

Police

Emergency T 000, general enquiries **T** 9690 4960. **City of Sydney Police Station**, 192 Day St, **T** 9265 6499.

Post offices

Post Shops, dotted around the city, are marked with a prominent red and white circular logo. The main **General Post Office** is at 159 Pitt St (Martin Place), **T** 131318. *Mon-Fri 0815-1730, Sat 1000-1400.*

Public holidays
New Years Day 1 Jan 2003, 1 Jan 2004; **Australia Day** 27 Jan 2003, 26 Jan 2004; **Good Friday** 18 Apr 2003, 9 Apr 2004; **Easter Saturday** 19 Apr 2003, 10 Apr 2004; **Easter Monday** 21 Apr 2003, 12 Apr 2004; **Anzac Day** 25 Apr 2003, 26 Apr 2004; **Queen's Birthday** 9 Jun 2003, 14 Jun 2004; **Bank Holiday** 4 Aug 2003, 2 Aug 2004; **Labour Day** 6 Oct 2003, 4 Oct 2004; **Christmas Day** 25 Dec 2003, 25 Dec 2004; **Boxing (Proclamation) Day** 26 Dec 2003, 27 Dec 2004.

Religious services
Check the Yellow Pages for local times, www.yellowpages.com.au

Smoking
Illegal in restaurants, cafés and pubs where eating is a primary activity, and on public transport.

Taxi firms
Legion, **T** 131451; **ABC**, **T** 132522; **Taxis Combined**, **T** 8332 8888; **Premier**, **T** 131017.

Telephone
Most internet outlets, newsagents and grocery stores advertise a copious number of cheap **international phone cards**, claiming to have rates to far-flung countries for as little as 9c per minute. Be careful of these claims, since most are based on off-peak times and are dependent on the location from which you call. Read the small print. Set rates in phone booths in internet outlets are a good bet, but lack privacy. Dual band mobile phones work in Sydney.

Time
Sydney operates on Eastern Standard Time, GMT+10 hrs (all other states). Daylight saving applies when clocks are put forward 1 hr between Oct and Mar.

Tipping

Tipping in Sydney is appreciated but not expected. In cafés and restaurants around 10% is satisfactory. Taxi drivers may give the impression that tipping is the norm, but it is not.

Toilets

Free public toilets can usually be found in public parks or adjacent to the tourist office or town hall. Also, at most bus and train stations, national parks and roadhouses, www.toiletmap.gov.au

Transport enquiries

Sydney Transport Infoline, **T** 131500, www.sta.nsw.gov.au

Travel agents

The major travel agents have numerous branches throughout the city including American Express Travel Level 5, 89 York St, **T** 9279 1233, Flight Centre 14/580 George St, **T** 9267 2999, STA Travel 855 George St, **T** 9212 1255. Others include Australian Travel Specialists Quay 6, Circular Quay, **T** 9252 0401, Backpackers Travel Centre 87 Glebe Point Rd, Glebe, **T** 9552 4544. The YHA have their own travel offices at the Central Hostel, Rawson Pl, **T** 9281 9444 and 422 Kent St, **T** 9261 1111.

Visas

See box, p28 and www.immi.gov.au/visitors

Water

Safe to drink, but as a precious resource use sparingly at all times.

Weather

Forecasts: **T** 1900 926113, www.bom.gov.au

Weights and measures

All metric.

A sprint through history

40,000–60,000BC	Long before the beautiful coves and inlets of Sydney Harbour embrace the arrival of the first European settlers, a very much older colony is established in the region by the Eora Aboriginals.
1770	With the relative success of Captain Cook's voyage of discovery along the eastern coast of Australia in 1770, King George III of England decides the potential 'new lands' would make a good colony, and initially an ideal jail.
1778	Six vessels carrying about 300 crew and 800 convicts, under the command of Captain Arthur Phillip, set sail from Portsmouth. The voyage takes 36 weeks, with the loss of less than 50 lives. On 18th January 1788 the 'First Fleet' sails in to Botany Bay, south of Sydney Harbour, the site of Cook's first landing. Much to Phillip's dismay it is far from the 'ideal' site Cook had reported it to be. There is no water and little shelter, but at least the 'natives' are amiable. After pondering their predicament, and a brief and totally unexpected liaison with French explorer La Perouse, Phillip moves north and enters Port Jackson (Sydney Harbour), named in 1770 by Cook. Finding it eminently more suitable, Phillip names the anchorage Sydney Cove, after British Secretary of State Viscount Sydney and Phillips himself is quickly sworn in as the first Governor of the newly proclaimed state of New South Wales.
1779	Initial attempts at settlement prove disastrous; the crew is ill prepared, poorly supplied and unskilled in

utilizing any local resources. The Eora Aboriginals find the invaders perplexing, almost amusing, and the settlers' superior attitude and the new diseases they have brought with them begin to drastically reduce Aboriginal numbers. Meanwhile the hopeless new penal colony tries unsuccessfully to grow crops and teeters on the brink of starvation.

1790   The discovery of more favourable soils further up the harbour at Parramatta turns despair to hope.

1790-1810 Sydney develops and grows with the arrival of more convicts and the parole of others. With the departure of the weary new governor, power-hungry soldiers (known as the New South Wales Corps), left in charge of the convicts, take advantage of the administrative vacuum and the sheer distance from the homelands and grant each other rights to secure tracts of land and use convict labour for its development. In the absence of money rum becomes the currency of choice, earning the new 'mafia' the nickname – the 'Rum Corps'. England's first attempt to restore official order in the form of Captain Bligh (of 'Mutiny on the Bounty' fame) fails and it takes the new Scottish governor Lachlan Macquarie to restore order to a colony he describes as adhering to a system of 'infantile imbecility'. A great planner and a fair man, Macquarie is instrumental in the transformation of the established colony from a insignificant port, built on base of local exploitation, to a progressive society earning international recognition.

1840	The transportation of convicts (many of whom had by now been relocated from Sydney) to New South Wales is abolished.
1850	New farms and settlements are now dotted around the region and explorers Lawson, Blaxland and Wentworth find a way through the seemingly impenetrable Blue Mountains, opening up the west of the state to settlement.
1851	The discovery of gold near Bathurst, west of the Blue Mountains, almost doubles the population of Sydney within a single decade to around 100,000.
1890	The population is now around 370,000. Inequalities in wealth create a whole range of social problems from rampant disease and deprivation to widespread alcoholism and crime. Racial disharmony and the disintegration of Aboriginal culture become major problems.
1901	Federation and the creation of the Commonwealth of Australia.
1927-1950	Canberra, the nation's new capital, is established. Sydney reluctantly takes a back seat in the affairs of the nation. First and second world wars come and go and immigration increases rapidly creating a truly cosmopolitan city, increasingly proud of its lifestyle. The first of Sydney's two famous icons, the Sydney Harbour Bridge, is completed in 1932.
1950-1970	The infant nation struggles to find its own identity and disenfranchise itself from its colonial past. In many ways both the nation, and Sydney in particular, seems insecure and although grateful to

England, becomes increasingly eager to take flight towards its own destiny. Aboriginals are granted the vote and are included in census figures.

1973 With the completion of the Opera House, the inevitable consolidation of its population and its emerging character, gradually Sydney was well on course to becoming one of the best-loved and most dynamic cities in the world.

1978 Sydneysiders' tolerance is put to the test with the gay community's first Mardis Gras. Trouble ensues.

1988 Sydney celebrates its bicentennial in the shadow of Aboriginal protest.

1993 The 2000 Olympic Games are awarded to Sydney.

1994 Bush fires ravage the surrounding national parks and outer suburbs, 7 lives and 400 homes are lost.

1998-2000 With massive amounts of money being spent on the city in preparations to stage the 2000 Olympics and their subsequent and undeniable success, the image of the city and the nation is further enhanced. Now, both Sydney and Australia have matured together to become one of the most desirable places to live and to visit on the planet. Ironically however a national referendum on a proposal to make Australia a republic is defeated. It seems old habits die hard.

2001-2002 While the Australian Government pledges almost unbridled support for the United States after the 11 September terrorist attacks, bush fires once again decimate the city fringes and the surrounding national parks.

Art and architecture

60,000BC-1777 Aboriginals establish themselves in the Sydney region and create rock paintings and stone carvings. Fine examples of Aboriginal rock paintings and carvings can be seen on the Echidna and Basin Tracks in the Ku-ring-gai National Park, Grotto Point in the Sydney Harbour National Park and Jibbon in the Royal National Park.

1778-1800 Captain Arthur Phillip, commander of the 'First Fleet', sails in to Port Jackson (named in 1770 by Captain James Cook) and builds the first European-style buildings, including the first Governor's Residence in 1790. The foundations of Governor Phillips residence were unearthed by archaeologists under the present day Museum of Sydney in 1983.

1816 Sydney's oldest remaining building, Cadman's Cottage, forms part of the developing colonial settlement in The Rocks (Port Jackson).

1790s After the failure of Port Jackson to produce sustainable crops, more fertile soils are discovered in Parramatta. Several farms with colonial-style cottages are established including Elizabeth Farm (1793) and Experiment Farm Cottage (1792). Old Government House (1799), also built in Parramatta, is used by the colony's first governors until relocation to Sydney on Macquarie Street in 1845.

Early 19th century With the departure of Governor Phillip, Scotsman Lachlan Macquarie takes over and becomes instrumental in the transformation of the colony into a progressive society. He uses the skills of former convict and architect Francis Greenway and uses convict labour to create several of the city's oldest remaining buildings, including the Hyde Park Barracks (1819) and the Sydney Hospital (1811).

1830s   The architect John Verde is influential throughout the city, creating buildings like the Greek Revival-style Elizabeth Bay House (1839).

late 1800s   Notable buildings dominate the emerging city's skyline, including the Town Hall (1868), St Mary's Cathedral (1882), Andrew's Cathedral (1868), the Queen Victoria Building (1898) and the Strand Arcade (1892).

Having been colonized during the century of Romanticism in Western Europe, when interest in the natural world was at its height, much of the earliest colonial art came from scientific expeditions and specimen drawings. Most of these early images look slightly odd, as if draughtsmen were unable to capture the strange forms of unique Australian species such as the kangaroo. Art from the whole of the first colonial century portrays Australia in a soft northern hemisphere light and in the rich colours of European landscapes. Given the violence and contempt afforded to the Aboriginal people at the time and the British impression that the new colony was a brutish place full of convicts, these paintings can be seen as an attempt to portray Australia as peaceful, beautiful and civilized. Things only began to change in the 1880s and 1890s, by which time a majority of colonists had been born in Australia.

1900-1950 After Federation in 1901 Australian landscapes become increasingly pretty and idyllic, typified by the languorous beauties enjoying the outdoors in the work of E Phillips Fox or Rupert Bunny. However, the trauma of the Great War had a cataclysmic effect on the art world and Australian artists once more followed the lead of Britain and Europe in embracing modernism. Gradually however, Australian artists really begin to look at their environment and cast away conventional techniques, prompting a dramatic change in how the country is portrayed. Truth in light, colour and tone is pursued by artists such as Arthur Streeton, Charles Conder, Tom Roberts and Frederick McCubbin, who began painting *en plein air*. In their paintings bright light illuminates the country's real colours; the gold of dried grass, the smoky green of eucalypts and the deep blue of the Australian sky.

1932 The Sydney Harbour Bridge is completed.

1960-1980 Australian artists are influenced by the abstract movement. Artists such as John Olsen and Fred Williams still produce landscapes but in an intensely personal, emotional and unstructured way. Brett Whiteley paints sensuous, colour-drenched Sydney landscapes and disturbing works such as the *Christie Series* (1964) in a surreal or distorted manner reminiscent of Salvador Dali or Francis Bacon. Painting becomes a less dominant form in this period with many artists working in sculpture, installations, video and photography.

1973

Dane Joern Utzon's blueprint wins an international competition for the Sydney Opera House and incorporates building techniques never tried before. After a torrid creation, resulting in Utzon's resignation and a building sum $95 million over budget, the great icon finally opens in 1973.

1980s and '90s

The 80s and 90s are marked by an intense interest in Aboriginal art, leading to its inclusion within the mainstream venues and discourse of contemporary Australian art. Sydney-based modernist painters like Ken Done dominate the art market in Sydney, while photographers Ken Duncan and Peter Lik lead the way in Australian landscape photography.

1981

The Sydney Tower opens, becoming the highest structure in Australasia, (before the Sky Tower in Auckland takes over in 1995).

1988

Darling Harbour is redeveloped and revitalised to celebrate the city's bicentenary with stark and modern architecture especially designed to enhance the increasingly popular public space.

1990-2000

Massive amounts of money are spent on the city in preparation for staging the 2000 Olympics, including several stunning sports venues at Olympic Park, Homebush Bay. The structures incorporate some of the most innovative architecture in the world.

Books

Autobiography and biography

James, **Clive**, *Unreliable Memoirs* (Picador, 1984) One of Australia's best-loved celebrities, novelists and broadcasters offers an entertaining insight in to his Sydney childhood.

Phelan, **Nancy**, *Setting Out on the Voyage*. (University of Queensland Press, 1998) The adventures of the author from her idyllic harbourside home to wartime Britain.

Fiction

Alderson, **Maggie**, *Pants on Fire* (Penguin, 2001) Entertaining, modern, *Bridget Jones's Diary*-style 'chick- novel'. Set in Sydney, it follows the life and loves of magazine editor Georgina Abbott.

Carey, **Peter**, *Oscar and Lucinda* (1990), *Bliss* (1981), *Illywhacker* (1985), *Jack Maggs* (1998) and *The True History of the Kelly Gang* (2001), all Faber and Faber, and *Thirty Days in Sydney* (Bloomsbury, 2001). Classics from the Australian Booker Prize-winning novelist.

Park, **Ruth**, *Harp in the South* (1951; Penguin, 2001) Tale of one family's struggle against inner-city poverty set in the 1940s.

Park, **Ruth,** *Playing Beatie Bow* (1980; Barn Owl Books, 2001) Children's fiction set in Sydney.

Food and entertainment

Evans and **Hudson**, *Sydney Morning Herald Good Food Guide* (annual) The most reliable guide to the city's best restaurants.

Redenbach, **Keith** and **Karl**, *Sydney Good Bar Guide* (annual) Glossy guide to some of the city's best bars.

History

Hughes, **Robert**, *The Fatal Shore* (1987; Vintage, 2003) A classic account of the arrival of Europeans in Australia.

Flannery, **Tim** (ed), *The Birth of Sydney* (Avalon, 2000) Early Sydney through the eyes of First Fleeters, explorers and dignitaries.

Sayer, **Mandy** and **Nowra**, **Louis**, *In the Gutter, Looking at the Stars*. An anthology of poetry and prose focusing on 200 years of life in Sydney's best-known suburb – Kings Cross.

Travel and reference

Bryson, **Bill**, *Down Under* (Black Swan, 2001) A no-holds-barred look at Australia from the master of entertaining travel writing, including his long-awaited visit to the country's true capital.

Cockington, **James**, *Secret Sydney* (New Holland, 2001) Walks guide featuring quirks and oddities around the city.

Park, **Ruth**, *Ruth Park's Sydney* (Duffy & Snellgrove, 2000) Updated version of the famous novelist's 1960s guide to Sydney.

Smith, **Seana**, *Sydney for Under Fives* (Pan Macmillan, 2001) A comprehensive look at entertaining toddlers in Sydney.

Toghill, **Jeff**, *Walking Sydney* (New Holland, 2000) User-friendly guide to numerous trails within the city.

Index

Credits

Footprint credits

Text editor: Julius Honnor
Series editor: Rachel Fielding

Production: Jo Morgan, Mark Thomas,
Davina Rungasamy
In-house cartography: Claire Benison,
Kevin Feeney, Robert Lunn,
Sarah Sorensen
Proof-reading: Caroline Lascom

Design: Mytton Williams
Maps: Footprint

Photography credits

Front cover: Alamy
Inside: Darroch Donald
Generic images: John Matchett
Back cover: Darroch Donald

Print

Manufactured in Italy by LegoPrint

Publishing information

Footprint Sydney
1st edition
Text and maps © Footprint Handbooks
Ltd March 2003

ISBN 1903471 61 3
CIP DATA: a catalogue record for this
book is available from the British Library

® Footprint Handbooks and the Footprint
mark are a registered trademark of
Footprint Handbooks Ltd

Published by Footprint Handbooks
6 Riverside Court
Lower Bristol Road
Bath, BA2 3DZ, UK
T +44 (0)1225 469141
F +44 (0)1225 469461
E discover@footprintbooks.com
W www.footprintbooks.com

Distributed in the USA by
Publishers Group West

Complete title list

Latin America & Caribbean

Latin America & Caribbean
Argentina
Barbados (P)
Bolivia
Brazil
Caribbean Islands
Central America & Mexico
Chile
Colombia
Costa Rica
Cuba
Cusco & the Inca Trail
Dominican Republic
Ecuador & Galápagos
Handbook
Guatemala Handbook
Havana (P)
Mexico
Nicaragua
Peru
Rio de Janeiro
South American
Handbook
Venezuela

North America

Vancouver (P)
Western Canada

Africa

Cape Town (P)
East Africa
Libya
Marrakech &
the High Atlas
Morocco
Namibia
South Africa
Tunisia
Uganda

Middle East

Egypt
Israel
Jordan
Syria & Lebanon

Asia

Bali
Bangkok & the Beaches
Cambodia
Goa
India
Indian Himalaya
Indonesia
Laos
Malaysia
Myanmar (Burma)
Nepal
Pakistan
Rajasthan & Gujarat
Singapore
South India
Sri Lanka
Sumatra
Thailand
Tibet
Vietnam

Australasia

Australia
New Zealand
Sydney (P)
West Coast Australia

Europe

Andalucía
Barcelona
Berlin (P)
Bilbao (P)
Bologna (P)
Copenhagen (P)
Croatia
Dublin (P)
Edinburgh (P)
England
Glasgow
Ireland
London
Madrid (P)
Naples (P)
Northern Spain
Paris (P)
Reykjavik (P)
Scotland
Scotland Highlands &
Islands
Spain
Turkey

(P) denotes pocket
Handbook

Publishing stuff

For a different view…
choose a Footprint

Over 80 Footprint travel guides
Covering more than 145 of the world's most exciting
countries and cities in Latin America, the Caribbean, Africa, Indian
sub-continent, Australasia, North America, Southeast Asia, the
Middle East and Europe.

Discover so much more…
The finest writers. In-depth knowledge. Entertaining and accessible.
Critical restaurant and hotels reviews. Lively descriptions of all the
attractions. Get away from the crowds.

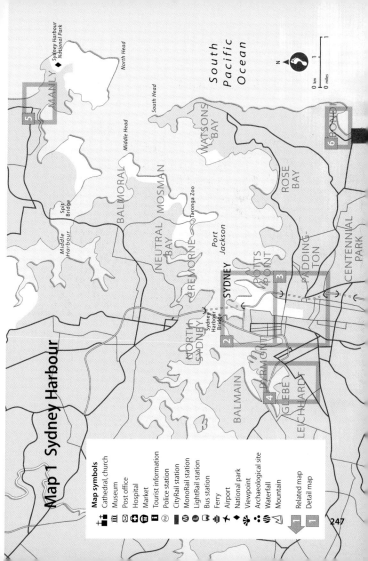

Map 1 Sydney Harbour

Map symbols

- ✠ Cathedral, church
- 🏛 Museum
- ⊠ Post office
- ✚ Hospital
- 🅿 Market
- ℹ Tourist information
- 🚓 Police station
- Ⓜ CityRail station
- Ⓜ MonoRail station
- Ⓛ LightRail station
- 🚌 Bus station
- ⛴ Ferry
- ✈ Airport
- ♦ National park
- ❋ Viewpoint
- ⚒ Archaeological site
- 🏞 Waterfall
- ⛰ Mountain

1 Related map
1 Detail map

South Pacific Ocean

North Head

Sydney Harbour National Park

Middle Harbour

Spit Bridge

BALMORAL

Middle Head

South Head

MOSMAN

NEUTRAL BAY

CREMORNE

Taronga Zoo

WATSONS BAY

Port Jackson

ROSE BAY

PADDING-TON

CENTENNIAL PARK

SYDNEY

POTTS POINT

Sydney Harbour Bridge

NORTH SYDNEY

BALMAIN

PYRMONT

GLEBE

LEICHHARDT

N

0 km   1
0 miles 1

247

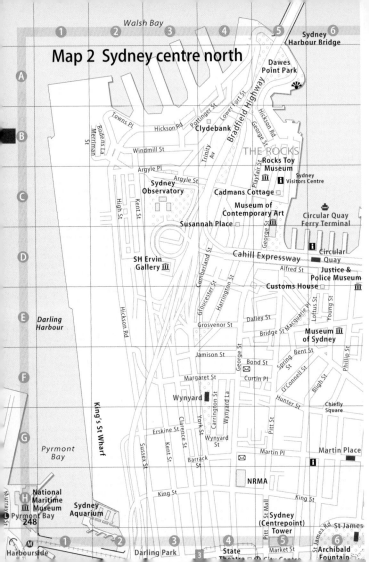

Map 2 Sydney centre north

Walsh Bay

Sydney Harbour Bridge

Dawes Point Park

Bradfield Highway

Hickson Rd

Lower Fort St

Pottinger St

George St

Towns Pl

Merriman St

Bodens La

Clydebank

THE ROCKS

Windmill St

Trinity Av

Argyle Pl

Rocks Toy Museum

Playfair St

Sydney Visitors Centre

Argyle St

Sydney Observatory

Cadmans Cottage

High St

Kent St

Museum of Contemporary Art

Circular Quay Ferry Terminal

Susannah Place

George St

SH Ervin Gallery

Cahill Expressway

Circular Quay

Alfred St

Justice & Police Museum

Cumberland St

Harrington St

Gloucester St

Customs House

Darling Harbour

Hickson Rd

Dalley St

Loftus St

Macquarie Pl

Young St

Grosvenor St

Bridge St

Museum of Sydney

Jamison St

George St

Bond St

Spring St

Bent St

Phillip St

Margaret St

Curtin Pl

O'Connell St

Bligh St

Wynyard

Chiefly Square

Hunter St

King's St Wharf

Clarence St

Carrington St

Wynyard La

York St

Pitt St

Erskine St

Wynyard St

Pyrmont Bay

Kent St

Barrack St

Sussex St

Martin Pl

Martin Place

King St

NRMA

National Maritime Museum

King St

Pyrmont Bay

Sydney Aquarium

St Mall

Sydney (Centrepoint) Tower

Market St

St James Rd

St James

248

M

Harbourside

Darling Park

State Theatre

City Center

Archibald Fountain

Pitt St

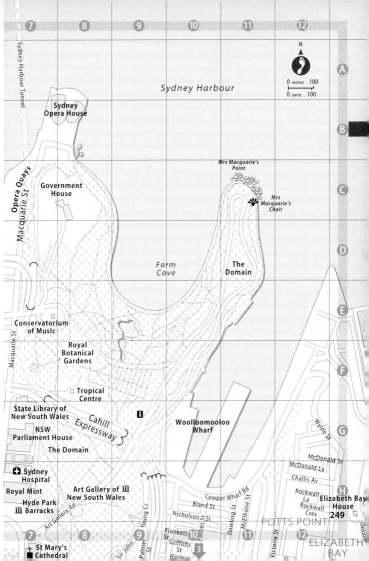

N

0 metres 100
0 yards 100

Ⓐ
Ⓑ
Ⓒ
Ⓓ
Ⓔ
Ⓕ
Ⓖ
Ⓗ

Sydney Harbour Tunnel

Sydney Harbour

Sydney
Opera House

Opera Quays

Macquarie St

Government
House

Mrs Macquarie's
Point

Mrs
Macquarie's
Chair

*Farm
Cove*

The Domain

Conservatorium
of Music

Macquarie St

Royal Botanical
Gardens

Tropical
Centre

State Library of
New South Wales

Cahill
Expressway

ℹ

Woolloomooloo
Wharf

NSW
Parliament House

The Domain

Sydney Hospital

Royal Mint

Hyde Park
Barracks

Art Gallery of
New South Wales

Wylde St

McDonald St
McDonald La

Challis Av

Rockwall
La
Rockwall
Cres

Elizabeth Bay
House **249**

Onslow

Cowper Wharf Rd

Bland St

Nicholson St

Dowling St

McElhone St

Victoria St

POTTS POINT

Art Gallery Rd

Sir John Young Cr

Palmer St

Plunkett
St
Griffiths
St
Harmer

Forbes St

ELIZABETH
BAY

St Mary's
Cathedral

➂

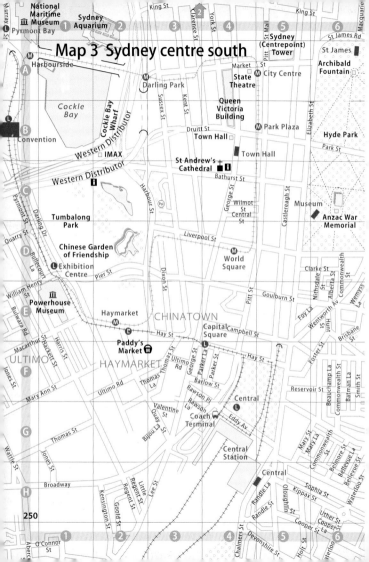

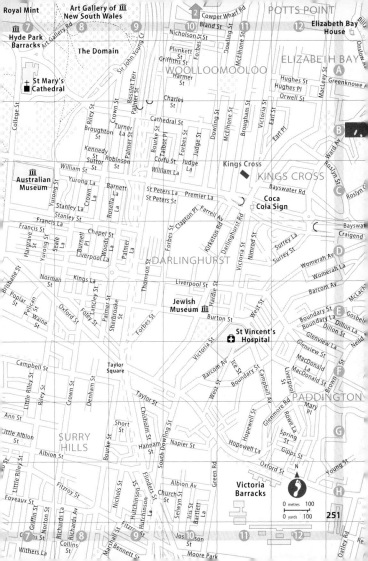

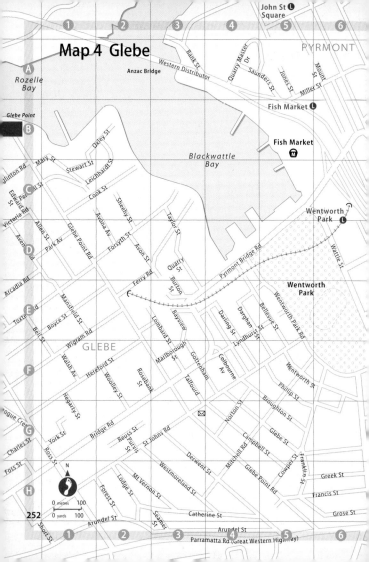

Map 4 Glebe

PYRMONT

John St Square

Rozelle Bay

Anzac Bridge

Western Distributor

Bank St

Quarry Master Dr

Saunders St

Jones St

Mount St

Miller St

Glebe Point

Fish Market

Fish Market

Oxley St

Stewart St

Leichhardt St

Blackwattle Bay

Mary St

Ellinton Rd

Carl St

Edward St

Cook St

Victoria Rd

Avenue

Allen St

Park Av

Glebe Point Rd

Sheehy St

Avona Av

Forsyth St

Taylor St

Avon St

Quarry St

Wentworth Park

Arcadia Rd

Ferry Rd

Burton St

Pyrmont Bridge Rd

Wattle St

Mansfield St

Wentworth Park

Toxte

Boyce St

Bayview St

Darling St

Darghan St

Lyndhurst St

Bellevue St

Wentworth Park Rd

Bell St

Wigram Rd

GLEBE

Lombard St

Marlborough St

Gottenham

Colbourne Av

Wentworth St

Walsh Av

Hereford St

Woolley St

Rosebank St

Talfourd

Phillip St

Broughton St

Hegarty St

Bridge Rd

Reuss St

Purves St

St Johns Rd

Norton St

Glebe St

Campbell St

Cowper St

Franklin St

Rogue Creek

York St

Ross St

Derwent St

Mitchell St

Glebe Point Rd

Greek St

Charles St

Foss St

N

Mt Vernon St

Westmoreland St

Francis St

Lodge St

Forest St

0 metres 100

0 yards 100

252

Short St

Arundel St

Seamer St

Catherine St

Arundel St

Parramatta Rd (Great Western Highway)

Grose St

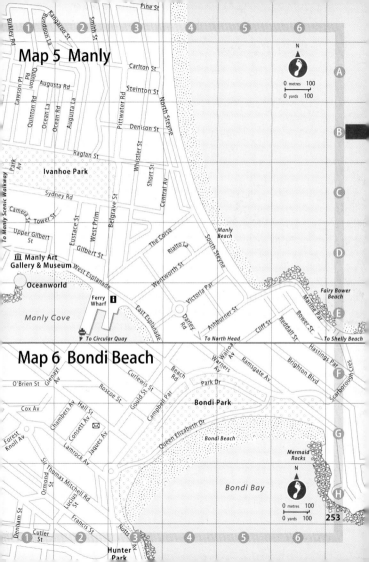

Map 5 Manly

Birkley Rd · Kangaroo St · Landoon La · Smith St · Pine St

Carlton St

Steinton St

Augusta Rd

Lawson Pl · Quinto Rd · Quinton Rd · Ocean La · Ocean Rd · Augusta La

Pittwater Rd

North Steyne

Denison St

Raglan St

Park Av

Ivanhoe Park

Sydney Rd

Camera La · Tower St · Upper Gilbert St

Eustace St · West Prim · Belgrave St

Whistler St · Short St · Central Av

Gilbert St

The Corso

Rialto La

Manly Beach

To Manly Scenic Walkway

🏛 **Manly Art Gallery & Museum**

West Esplanade

Wentworth St

South Steyne

Oceanworld

Ferry Wharf ℹ

East Esplanade

Victoria Par

Darley Rd

Ashburner St

Fairy Bower Beach

Marine Par

Cliff St · Reddall St · Bower St

Manly Cove

⛴ To Circular Quay

To North Head

Hastings Par

To Shelly Beach

N

0 metres 100
0 yards 100

Ⓐ Ⓑ Ⓒ Ⓓ Ⓔ

Map 6 Bondi Beach

O'Brien St · Glenayr Av

Curlewis St

Beach Rd

Warroa St · Warners Av

Ramsgate Av

Cox Av

Roscoe St

Gould St

Campbell Par

Park Dr

Bondi Park

Brighton Blvd

Scarborough Cres

Forest Knoll Av

Chambers Av · Hall St · Consett Av · Jaques Av

Lamrock Av

Queen Elizabeth Dr

Bondi Beach

Sir Thomas Mitchell Rd · Ormond St · Lucius St

Denham St · Cutler St

Francis St

Notts Av

Hunter Park

Mermaid Rocks

Bondi Bay

N

0 metres 100
0 yards 100

Ⓕ Ⓖ Ⓗ

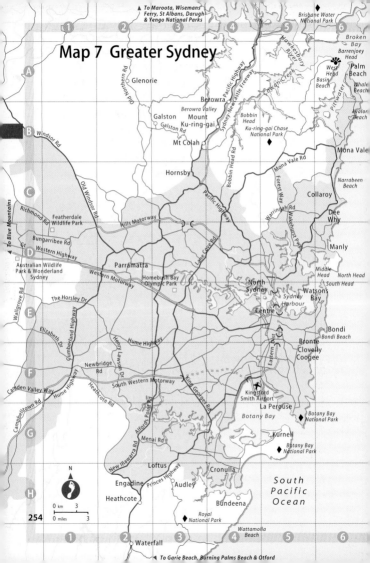

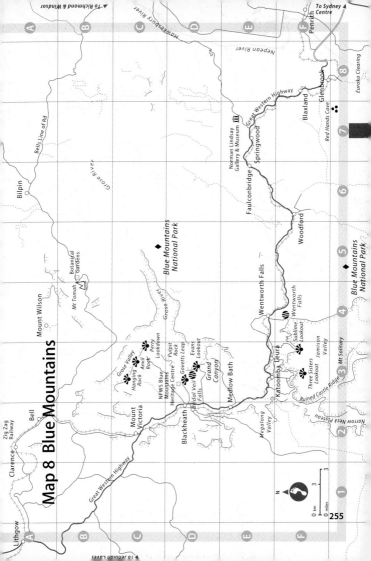

Map 8 Blue Mountains

Sydney Ferries

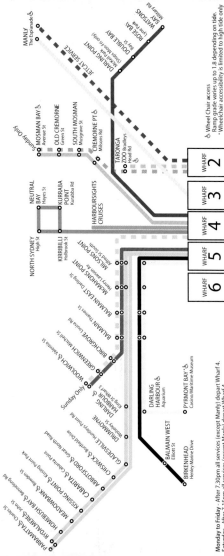

256

MANLY
The Esplanade ♿

JETCAT SERVICE
(Depart 6am-7pm only)

DARLING POINT
Mckell Park

DOUBLE BAY
Bay St

ROSE BAY
Lyne Park

WATSONS BAY
Military Rd

MOSMAN BAY ♿
Avenue St

OLD CREMORNE
Green St

SOUTH MOSMAN
Musgrave St

CREMORNE PT ♿
Milsons Rd

Sunday only

TARONGA
ZOO ♿ Bradleys
Head Rd ♿

NEUTRAL
BAY
Hayes St

KURRABA
POINT
Kurraba Rd

HARBOURSIGHTS
CRUISES

NORTH SYDNEY
High St

KIRRIBILLI
Holbrook St

MILSONS POINT
Alfred St South

McMAHONS POINT
Henry Lawson Av

BALMAIN EAST
Darling St

BALMAIN ♿ Thames St

BIRCHGROVE ♿ Louisa Rd

GREENWICH ♿ Mitchell St

WOOLWICH ♿ Valentia St

Sunday only

DARLING
HARBOUR ♿
Aquarium

PYRMONT BAY ♿
Casino/Maritime Museum

DRUMMOYNE
Wolseley St

DARLING
HARBOUR ♿
King St Wharf 3

Sunday only

CHISWICK ♿ Bortfield Drive

GLADESVILLE ♿ Punters Point Rd

ABBOTSFORD ♿ Great North Road

CABARITA ♿ Cabarita Point

KISSING POINT ♿ Kissing Point Park

MEADOWBANK ♿ Bowden St

HOMEBUSH BAY ♿ Bennelong Rd

RYDALMERE ♿ John St

PARRAMATTA Charles St

BALMAIN WEST
Elliott St

BIRKENHEAD
Henley Marine Drive

WHARF 2

WHARF 3

WHARF 4

WHARF 5

WHARF 6

CIRCULAR QUAY FERRY TERMINAL ♿

♿ Wheel Chair access
· Ramp grade varies up to 1.8 depending on tide.
· Wheelchair accessibility is limited to high tide only

© Copyright State Transit April 2002

Monday to Friday - After 7.30pm all services (except Manly) depart Wharf 4.
Saturday - After 7.15pm all services (except Manly) depart Wharf 4.

Sydney Ferries information Office located opposite Wharf 4, Circular Quay.